Tim and Darlene

God bless you both
in your joining with Jesus

John D. Wilson

In Other Worlds

John D Wilson

WestBow Press books may be ordered through booksellers or by contacting:

WestBow Press
A Division of Thomas Nelson & Zondervan
1663 Liberty Drive
Bloomington, IN 47403
www.westbowpress.com
1 (866) 928-1240

ISBN: 978-1-4908-5553-0 (sc)
ISBN: 978-1-4908-5552-3 (hc)
ISBN: 978-1-4908-5554-7 (e)

Library of Congress Control Number: 2014917939

Printed in the United States of America.

WestBow Press rev. date: 10/27/2014

DEDICATION

This book is dedicated to the memory of my parents Jim and Margaret Wilson who lived full and fruitful lives to the benefit of others and the glory of God. They should have had a book of their own—they certainly had the stories to recount and the experiences to share, and I learned so much from them.

ACKNOWLEDGEMENTS

I am grateful for the blessings and joys which my own family has brought me: the tolerant, faithful and loving support of Gloria for more than forty years, and the times of fun, laughter and stimulating mealtime discussions with our sons Jonathan, Malcolm and Iain—not to mention an occasional sharp witticism to bring their father down to size! They each endured my shortcomings as a husband and father and, without much say in the matter, shared in our adventures in sundry places. Through it all, we were shaped and nurtured together as a family in Papua—the place they call home.

I also owe a debt to many friends, throughout different stages of my life, who played and argued with me, encouraged, teased, and provoked me, set an example and prayed for me, gave advice and taught me. I cannot name them all, but I would not be the person I am without them.

I certainly include in my gratitude the Yali people of Papua, who taught me things I would never have known if I had stayed all my life in Scotland. My life with them was an unparalleled experience that enriched me and in many ways transformed me.

Thanks and glory to God who has blessed me in every place, in each different culture or community, and in every circumstance.

FOREWORD BY DON RICHARDSON

Some explorers probe the domain of remote tribes merely out of curiosity. Others, Cortez-like, intrude to exploit and enslave. Rare are those who trace the furthest-out-there branchings of mankind to bestow the finest treasure of all—the love of God and the saving grace of Jesus Christ. So often, a Cortez arrives first and inflicts trauma, but that was not to be the destiny of Papua's Yali people. The story you hold in your hands narrates a remarkable exception to a recurring theme of woe in the history of first contact with tribal people.

Like every other vulnerable minority on earth, Papua's remote Yali people were about to learn very abruptly that the world was no longer big enough to guarantee their isolation. Apart from sufficiently resourceful advocates like author John Wilson and his family, the sudden intrusion of modernity amid a culture unchanged after eons of time could be tragically disorienting. As if this engaging saga were not suspenseful enough, many warriors of the tribe—fiercely hostile cannibals—had already proved willing to wound, kill and even *devour* the very advocates whose help they needed most.

Yet John and Gloria Wilson, fully aware of the grim fate that had befallen two predecessors, ventured among the Yali with a firstborn son in their arms. Warmly welcomed by part of the tribe, they faced the daunting challenge of winning the minds and hearts of a stoically averse majority.

Right away, the Wilsons found themselves treating tropical diseases that could just as easily infect *them.* They tackled the task of learning a complex language from scratch. Putting Yali vocabulary to work, they had to arbitrate disputes that, left unresolved, could split households or precipitate war. And—just as the Yali had been doing for ages—they even had to learn to cope with earthquakes that could alter the landscape in a moment.

All the while, as John candidly admits, he faced his own inner struggle against doubts that kept taunting, *You are not adequate for this. You are in over your head. Give it up and go back to Scotland.*

Believe me, this is the kind of story where reading recaptures *experience.* Have plenty of tissues handy for the poignant ending. Most of all, make room for fresh incentives to devote the rest of your time on earth to fulfilling whatever God's will may be for you.

Don Richardson, author of *Peace Child* and *Lords of the Earth*

PREFACE

> *If I can tell the stories of my life artfully enough, then perhaps those who read them will, at the end of telling, be able to hear more of their own stories within.*
>
> Robert Benson[1]

We all like stories about the local boy who makes good, about the man who ran into a blazing house to rescue his neighbour or about people with humble origins like Nelson Mandela, Mother Theresa, Rosa Parks and Terry Fox, who triumphed over adversity and made life-changing differences for others.

Stories like that give us hope. They remind us of what it is to be human, and that each of us can make a difference within our sphere of influence, like the expanding circle of ripples from a tiny pebble dropped in a quiet pool. But we also find hope in the original obscurity of these humble folk, now heroes. We

---

1 Used with the author's permission. http://www.robertbensonwriter.com/

identify with them, and in our imaginations join vicariously in their journey through joy and pain, and enter into their disappointments and successes.

My life took me to places and cultures that might seem strange and obscure compared to modern Europe or urban America. On the other hand, they might be the very places of your dreams and imagination—the romantic highlands of Scotland, the windswept solitude of an island on the edge of the Atlantic, an idyllic life in an unexplored corner of New Guinea.

If you have ever left your familiar homeland to live and work abroad, or if you have migrated from your native land to find refuge somewhere in the West, you will empathize with the inevitable but unsettling experiences and emotions of cultural adjustment which I describe.

In Other Worlds also reveals things I learned and the personal changes that took place in the lifelong process of following Jesus. These different worlds were the context for the commonplace experiences of personal struggle, self-discovery and growth of someone seeking to be an obedient disciple and to grow in faith. These places were the context where I came to know God better.

NOTES ON PLACE AND PERSONAL NAMES

There are many names of people and places which may be hard to remember and also hard to pronounce. I have tried to keep these to a minimum, and I am mindful that some may sound strange, especially the Yali names. I chose to spell them as they are written today by the Yali people, but neither they nor I will be offended if you pronounce them in your own way or simply keep a picture of the word shape in your mind.

What today is called Papua[2] is a problem in itself for everyone. It is too easily confused with the nation of Papua New Guinea, which gained its independence from Australia in 1975. Papua, in Indonesia, is not a nation; it is the easternmost province of Indonesia. However, both Papua and Papua New Guinea share the same land mass—the second largest island in the world. The people are ethnically related and are all Papuans regardless of

---

2 Papua: Say Pah-poo-ah (not Pap-you-uh).

whether they live in the Indonesian province on the west side of the island or in the nation of Papua New Guinea on the east.

To confuse matters even more—and here we have to blame the colonial powers who divided up the island for their own reasons—different parts of the island went under other names in the past. The western part was colonized by the Dutch and therefore was still called Dutch New Guinea when I first heard about the earliest missionary work there. When the Indonesians took over the administration of this part they called it Irian Barat (or in English, West Irian). Later, however, they renamed it Irian Jaya (which means something like glorious or fortunate Irian). Finally, as the indigenous people seek to reinforce their ethnic identity, it has become known as Papua.

Heluk River Gorge near Holuwon

A DECISIVE DAY

The river thundered with a deafening roar as it hurtled pell-mell in its precipitous descent through the constraints of a rocky canyon. Its impetuous currents argued and tussled, tossing one another around unyielding rocks before continuing their quarrel.

On our side of the river, I stood among giant boulders with my Dutch-Canadian colleague Bruno de Leeuw and our companions—a band of Yali men armed with native bows and arrows, and three Indonesian policemen with their World-War-II-vintage Lee-Enfield rifles at the ready.

Opposite us, I occasionally caught glimpses of dark-skinned, well-armed warriors who moved furtively among the trees and scrub that clung to the near-vertical limestone wall of the gorge. Each man was outfitted with war paraphernalia: a shell band on his chest, a boar tusk through his nasal septum; a feather-and-fur headdress, and a fistful of assorted deadly arrows.

Between us was this impassable maelstrom of surging water—but no bridge. The unwelcoming party on the other side had anticipated our coming, slashed the vines binding their end of the bridge together, and pushed the loosened construction into the river. The roiling current had soon made matchwood of everything. If we wanted to get across, there had to be a bridge—not an easy thing to build without cooperation from the other side. Nevertheless, undaunted, our enterprising Yali companions were soon shouting instructions to each other and putting in motion preparations for erecting a new bridge.

"Watch out!" A Yali's shrill cry drew my attention as huge boulders started to tumble down the cliff opposite us. Crashing through trees and brush, they bounced off the rock face to land in the river near where our friends were working. Some even ricocheted off rocks in the river and made it all the way across or shattered into dangerous flying fragments. They sent a clear signal from the men on the other side: *Don't come here! Don't even think about building a bridge!*

As if that message wasn't plain enough, one of their men moved into the open. He wore the attire of a medicine man: upturned pig tusks through his nose, a band of cowry shells around his net-covered head, a large scoop-shaped bailer shell hanging on his chest, bow and arrows in his hand and a feathered net bag slung on his back. This contained the amulets and artefacts of his profession. He advanced and stepped onto a large outcrop of rock that formed the opposite bridgehead. Squatting, he pulled some objects and leaves from his net bag and began to chant incantations, impossible to hear above the river's roar. I wondered aloud, "What is he doing?"

One of my companions matter-of-factly explained, "He's making magic and perhaps putting a curse on us so that we won't be able to make a new bridge, or perhaps so that we'll fall in the river in the attempt."

At that moment, the nervous Indonesian patrol leader ordered his men, "Fire some shots over their heads." For an instant, the sharp rifle cracks echoed in the canyon but were soon overwhelmed by the unending thundering of the Heluk River.

Before we had set out for this encounter, one of my tribal friends had cautioned me with understated wisdom, "Put on two or three thick sweaters, my father,[3] so that when the arrows hit you they will not go in too deep!" The advice had seemed ridiculous at the time, but now it was no joke.

Amidst the noise, commotion and threat of the moment, my thoughts focused on my family. A mere twenty kilometers north as the crow flies, my wife Gloria sat in our small timber house perched on a hillside in a village called Ninia. From our home there was a spectacular view of the upper reaches of this same river valley, high up in Papua's central mountain range whose rugged

---

[3] When a Yali calls me "father" it is not necessarily a sign of special honour. They address everyone using relational terms: father, mother, brother, sister, aunt, brother-in-law and so forth.

backbone, thrust up by ancient seismic forces, ran from one end of New Guinea to the other. With her were our two young sons, the second only a few weeks old. I had good reason to imagine that our newborn and his brother might be left fatherless before the day was over. What was I doing here? What had brought us to this place? Were our hopes and ambitions to be dashed by the events unfolding in this hidden valley far from our homeland?

Gloria and I believed it was not by chance that we had come to live in this remote and inaccessible region of Indonesian New Guinea. We had not been seeking adventure or a unique and unusual experience in an exotic place. Honestly, I am the kind of person who prefers to stay with the familiar. We had not been coerced or duped into coming by someone with an ulterior agenda. We had made a deliberate personal choice to come here. In fact, we had obstinately overcome hurdles in order to become missionaries, and specifically, to come to these isolated mountain valleys.

Meanwhile, the Yali men on our side of the river busied themselves gathering poles and vines to build a new bridge across the raging torrent, while I sat down on a large boulder to watch. Here, I was helpless and useless—an ignorant novice among so-called primitive tribesmen who possessed a wealth of knowledge of their environment and a range of practical skills passed down from their ancestors. I could barely distinguish one tree from another, so was incapable of selecting the right kind of timber for bridge building. I had no idea where to find and harvest suitable rattan vines to bind the timbers together nor had I any clue about the engineering techniques they would employ.

My body shivered and goose bumps broke out on my arms and legs—not from cold at this altitude in the tropics, but from excitement mixed with raw fear. *Why am I frightened?* I asked myself. *Stupid question*, I responded silently. *Today I might die, that's why.*

The threat was real. Seven years earlier, in 1966, just a few kilometers up this same valley, an Australian missionary called Stan Dale, along with three Yali companions, had hiked south from Ninia to investigate the reported deaths of two of his young disciples, Yeikwaroho and Bingguok.

In the late afternoon, an extensive search in a side valley had confirmed that both their friends had been killed and cannibalized. Since it was then too late to return home, while the Yali men gathered firewood and scrounged a few sweet potatoes from a nearby garden plot for an evening meal, Stan started a fire in a vacant hut. Alone and illuminated by the flickering flame of the fire he had just lit, Stan was an easy target. He was ambushed by a volley of arrows fired through the open doorway. Five found their mark.

Stan's three Yali companions rushed to drive off the attackers and then helped him to his feet, supporting him as he painfully struggled up the rugged trail through the darkness. Dawn was breaking when they reached a village and sent a runner ahead to Stan's wife. Other villagers built a rustic litter of poles and leaves to carry him the remainder of the way to the mission post.

Two years after he recovered, Stan Dale and his American colleague Phil Masters were ambushed while exploring the next valley to the east. A hail of a hundred arrows felled them both, and they died there on a remote, rocky river beach. I had visited the spot and seen the broken arrows, the remnants of a man's boot, and a rusting wristwatch lying where the men had fallen at the river's edge.

This incident was vivid in my mind. The question nagged me, *Today, why am I afraid to die?* Obviously a few primitive arrows in my body were not going to leave nice clean wounds. Yet there was more to it than that, something more nebulous and hard to explain. Not only did I fear that my life could be snuffed out and my wife and children left without husband and father; even more than that, I dreaded the thought that my life would be frittered away for nothing—that it would end ignominiously and without consequence or meaning.

The fear was also mingled with doubt. *In reality I am questioning God—God, who I believed called me here*, I finally acknowledged. *I am doubting his wisdom, goodness and power to make of my life whatever will bring him glory.*

As a young man I had been captivated by Jesus's words, "If anyone would come after me, he must deny himself and take up his cross daily and follow me."[4] In my fresh unbridled enthusiasm as a young Christian I had taken hold of these words. This was what I wanted to do—follow Jesus regardless of where he led me.

Other words from the apostle Paul had become a personal motto: "Christ died for all, that those who live should no longer live for themselves but for him who died for them and was raised again."[5] This is what I really wanted, or at least I had thought I did—to live and, if necessary, die for Christ, who had died for me.

As a student I had read the account of the murder of the five missionaries to the Waodoni[6] Indians of Ecuador. Five men in their prime were slaughtered on a remote riverbank on the first day of what they believed was a major breakthrough towards creative contact with these belligerent people. One of those five men, Jim Elliot, had written, "He is no fool who gives what he cannot keep to gain that which he cannot lose."[7] Like Jim, I had garnered my motivation and direction from the words of Jesus, "Whoever finds his life will lose it, and whoever loses his life for my sake will find it."

---

4 Author's paraphrase of Luke 9:23.

5 Author's paraphrase of 2 Corinthians 5:15.

6 At that time, known as the Auca. See Elisabeth Elliott, *Through Gates of Splendor*, 1956/2005. Tyndale.

7 From the personal journal of Jim Elliott, October 28, 1949, cited in *Through Gates of Splendor*.

However, sitting trembling on that rock by the surging torrent, a stone's throw from armed and hostile warriors, I wasn't so sure. The commitment I had made while in the comfort and security of Scotland, my homeland, was now being tested by the blood-chilling reality of armed men waiting in the forest on the opposite side of the river.

Nevertheless, I was not here by accident. I believed God had chosen me, prepared me and brought me here. With his help, I had ignored the sceptics who had sarcastically questioned, "You? You a missionary?" With the conviction of God's call on my life and that naïve commitment of youthful enthusiasm, I had quit a career, undergone training and left my family and homeland. My wife Gloria and I had already overcome impediments to be here on this portentous day.

At that moment I felt convicted. *Lord, forgive me my fear and doubt and give me faith to follow you.* Suddenly, it was as if someone had pressed the mute button on the remote control. The sounds of the roaring river, crashing rocks, shouts of men and echoing gunshots were gone. Instead—both within and without—came an overwhelming peace, and then a quiet, calming voice spoke to me.

"No one will die today. All those who had to die for the sake of the gospel among the Yali—the Ninia men Yeikwaroho and Bingguok and the missionaries Stan and Phil—have died. But you will live and do the work I brought you here to do, and you will not leave until it is finished."

PART 1

SCOTLAND (1943-1971)

CHAPTER 1

A Skinny Scots Lad

As a little boy growing up in post-World-War-II Scotland, I was unremarkable—a skinny, shy asthmatic lad with bow legs. No one could ever have predicted that I would become a missionary to a Stone-Age tribe in one of the most emotionally taxing and physically demanding places in the world.

Like most other boys I had already had my occasional brushes with danger—those great escapes when the adults around you become convinced of the watchfulness of guardian angels! Against my mother's oft-repeated counsel, "Don't ride your tricycle around the corner, just stay on this road," one day I yielded to temptation and ventured beyond the boundary. We lived on a quiet street parallel to, but up the hill from, one of Edinburgh's busy main arteries.

No sooner had I rounded the corner than I found myself unexpectedly hurtling down the steep incline of Lygon Road, the sandstone houses on either side a gray blur in the corner of my eyes. My older brother Jeff happened to see me disappear into forbidden territory and sprinted after me, but wasn't able to catch me up and could only watch in horror as I reached the main road. Somehow the tricycle trundled between the trams and cars and finally came safely to a stop on the other side.

Jeff witnessed another close shave. A large sycamore tree had been professionally felled in our back garden, and though most of it was cleared away, a big stump and a few sizeable logs remained to form a nice fortress where my brothers and I liked to play. One day, Mum was watching through the kitchen window while I stood as king of the stump castle and Jeff chopped firewood nearby. Suddenly his axe head came off and Mum watched, helpless and heart-in-mouth, through the kitchen window as the blade flew towards me.

"John, look out!" Hearing my brother's shouted warning, I looked up in time to feel rather than see the axe blade swish past my head. I had no sense of the danger avoided. However, in the subsequent retelling of the story my mother insisted, "I saw the blade turn in the air, as if an unseen hand had diverted it!"

Another time, I was again playing in the tree fort, unaware that our own dog Corrie had buried a bone under one of the logs. When I bent down to pick up something, Corrie—jealously protecting his hidden treasure—unexpectedly sprang for my wrist and pulled me off balance. As I stumbled, the dog bit me again, further up the arm. It was all a blur, but I felt the searing pain where his incisors had punctured my flesh to the bone above the elbow. Mum watched it all in dismay from the kitchen. Then, as the dog leaped again and plunged its teeth into my upper arm, I became conscious of her shouts and one of my brothers beating the dog and pulling it off me.

Where was my guardian angel that day? Without the intervention of my brother, the next incision would have been my jugular. I know Mother "pondered these things in her heart" and wondered if God's hand was on my life in some unique way. Most people, however, only saw—if they noticed at all—a scrawny, wheezy and introverted little boy.

As a child, I didn't think of these as afflictions. In post-World-War-II Scotland, it was not uncommon to see scrawny lads with bow legs. It did mean, however, that I was regarded by my four brothers and my sister as the weakling of the family, and sometimes they would complain if two or three of us were sent on some errand on foot, saying, "Don't send John with us, he'll just hold us back."

On the other hand, I was determined to be part of any action or activity in which they engaged. Since my three older brothers played rugby at school, when I became old enough, so did I; and when they joined the Combined Cadet Force I also enrolled as soon as I could.

Whenever Dad went fishing, we'd pile into the car and go with him. Sometimes we would also fish for brown trout in the side streams, and on occasion we'd scramble up the nearby hills just to explore in the bracken or heather and see what we could see from the summit. Inevitably, I would end up trailing far behind my brothers and sister, gasping and wheezing, "Wait for me!"

There were no bronchial inhalers in those days, and I was forced to take a slower pace and pause for breath until I caught my second wind. But I never used asthma as an excuse not to join in, and in fact I often set out to prove I could go as fast and as far as any of them.

One summer, my sister Rose-Ellen, my younger brother Callan and I went with our parents to a rented holiday cottage near the village of Carsphairn in Kirkcudbrightshire, my father's birthplace. One weekend, my dad had to go back to Edinburgh on business, so on Sunday, with no transport to church in the village, Mother suggested the three of us walk. She had bad rheumatism, so would stay home and prepare our lunch.

We were unfazed by the idea of walking four miles there and back, but Callan and Rose-Ellen insisted, "Don't make us walk with John; he won't be able to keep up with us. Make him leave half an hour before us."

I was about fourteen at the time, but despite my objections that I could walk the distance as fast as them, Mother overruled me, and I was duly sent out a full half hour ahead of my sister and younger brother. It was arranged that whoever was first to reach the war memorial just outside the village would wait for the others, and so, on reaching it within the hour, I sat down to wait, noting the precise time on my watch. Exactly half an hour later, the two of them arrived.

"When did you get here?"

"Half an hour ago."

"We don't believe you," they replied scornfully. "We were walking flat out the whole way; you couldn't possibly be as quick."

After church, they sent me on ahead once again while they enjoyed a prearranged respite in a kind lady's house, where they drank tea and savoured home-baked scones and shortbread! Meanwhile, I was just passing the war memorial outside the village when a motorbike purred to a stop beside me. The helmeted and goggled rider inquired, "Are you the son of Mr. Wilson, staying in the cottage along the road here at Knowehead?"

"Yes, sir, I am."

"Hop on the back, then, and I'll give you a ride home!"

"Thank you, sir, I'd appreciate that!" I grinned with double delight, glad of not having to walk and savouring sweet revenge as I climbed onto the pillion seat.

It was one of life's triumphs when my brother and sister finally came home and mother confirmed that I had indeed been home for ages. But sadly, she let the cat out of the bag and spoiled the sweet savour of my secret victory. Nevertheless, I realized, *I may not be as physically strong or athletic as they are, but I am determined and today I have proved something to myself if not to them.* There was no doubt that I lacked brawn, but was I blessed with brains?

For some reason, my parents chose to have us all educated in two of Edinburgh's fee-paying or "public" schools. My sister was placed in a small, highly regarded school called Saint Margaret's, while my four brothers and I were enrolled in George Watson's Boys' College.

I am never quite sure whether or not the sacrifices and investment my parents made to give us this education were well placed. The school was good enough, I suppose, since many of its pupils have attained distinction in architecture, engineering, law, medicine, politics and science. However, the "Watson's" philosophy and methodology of education failed to see or develop the latent capability in some of us. My school report cards told a story of mediocrity and I ended my school life with no sense of academic potential and convinced that (as I had often been told) I would never amount to anything.

George Watson's College (used with permission)

In retrospect, I can see that I was not taught according to my learning style, but I readily acknowledge that this was probably quite typical for a school of its day. I remember the teachers as a mixed bag of personalities, ranging from affable tyrant to respected friend. Some of the older staff members were unique characters with fascinating quirks and foibles, seasoned with much good humour. I have fond memories of teachers like "Beaky" Gibson, "Tam" Coull, and "Scratchy" McInnes, who were very much a part of the school's fabric and history. For their part they were particularly proud to teach successive Wilson siblings, and in turn we revelled in their eccentricities and grew to appreciate and respect them.

However, there was one teacher I wish I had never met. When I turned eight years old and joined the class of Miss Sharpe[8], I had no idea what awaited me, but I was in for the worst year of my school days, with deep and lasting consequences.

Exerting her authority over thirty rambunctious Scottish schoolboys, she ordered us to sit alphabetically from A to W in rows of desks from front to back. That meant that I ended up at the very back corner on the left, seated next to Derek Wilson—no relation.

For some reason, Sharpy began to pick on me from that day on, or at least that's how it seemed to me. It became more sinister one day after an arithmetic test, when my namesake and I had identical answers. Without any justification she charged me with cheating. "Wilson," she challenged, her accusing gaze directed at me in the corner, "you must have cheated. You must have been sneaking a look at Derek's paper."

I couldn't believe my ears. To be honest, it had not yet occurred to me (or to Derek for that matter) that there might be some benefit in doing such a thing. All I could do was deny her baseless assertion.

On another occasion Miss Sharpe mysteriously, unjustly and unkindly charged me with cheating on a spelling test. It was

8 Bearing her no ill will, I have given her this pseudonym.

inexplicable! She had dictated the words we were supposed to have memorized in our homework the night before. Memorization by rote was not my forte, but my mother was a stickler for good grammar, good spelling and precise pronunciation, and perhaps I had also inherited some innate linguistic skill. Not only did I pass the test, I was the only boy in the class with every word spelled correctly. Imagine how proud I felt until Sharpy cross-examined me. "How could you possibly know how to spell 'temperature'?" she inquired with a sharp and suspicious tone.

"I simply spoke it out to myself as my mother would say it," I explained. "I just spelled it as it sounds, 'tem-per-a-ture'."

I waited in vain for congratulations, but instead, suspicion and aspersions were cast on my best efforts. I felt hurt and humiliated in front of the class.

All through that year, it seemed to me that nothing I could do was ever good enough to warrant any commendation, while any apparent or imagined failing was seized on with denigrating scorn or blown angrily out of proportion. The message to my young, wounded heart was that I could do nothing right, and trying wasn't worth taking the risk.

It was probably the first significant lie I believed about myself. In those early years, like all children, I was forming a sense of self-identity, and up to this point my experience at school—while not totally unpleasant—had not done a lot to build self-confidence or enhance my self-awareness. Consequently, I moved on through and eventually out of school with no expectation of being more than average and tacitly believing that I was incapable of any academic achievement.

CHAPTER 2

Out of the Family Closet

My tiny bedroom, a converted closet, was just big enough for a small bed where I could lie and watch the eyes of the carved owl clock move back and forth in time to the ticking pendulum. Dad thought of me as "the wise owl"—I suppose because I was somewhat introverted and thoughtful—and so my parents had given me the clock as a Christmas present. I liked the solitude of this cozy cubbyhole all to myself while my four brothers shared two other rooms.

Malcolm, Jeffrey and Robin came first. They were born in Belgian Congo, where our parents had been missionaries for a number of years, until the outbreak of the war in 1939, when they were repatriated to Scotland. Three of us were born in Scotland: my sister Rose-Ellen, then me, and just one year later my brother Callan, who in our early years was often mistaken as my twin.

John (right front) with his siblings (1948)

One of my brothers once commented, "We were not a loving family." However, at the time, I don't think we were atypical. The exigencies of the war years, the dour, stoical heritage of Calvinism, the no-nonsense pragmatic legacy of the Scottish Enlightenment, and no doubt other formative cultural, environmental and genetic factors, had left many Scots emotionally impassive and undemonstrative. I find it hard to recall many hugs and kisses from my parents, yet I believed I was loved and cared for, and as I grew older, felt a great fondness and sense of admiration for my "old folk," as we called them, and an intense pride in my immediate family. At various times we had our squabbles and fights, but we loyally stood up for and boasted about each other outside the family.

As the only girl among five brothers, my sister Rose-Ellen clearly had a special place in the family, but for her part, she wanted to enter into whatever the rest of us boys were up to. I remember us all going to the local park to play a made-up game of "gaining ground" with a rugby ball. We split into opposing teams and each in turn kicked the ball as far as we could, attempting to work our way down the field until we were in range to kick a goal. Rose-Ellen was as good as the rest of us. She could also pack a mean punch, but if one of us attempted to retaliate, we'd be sure to hear the sharp rebuke, "Boys, don't hit your sister!"

In time the tomboy became a teenager and began to display her feminine nature. As she developed into a young woman, we her brothers inevitably felt she was unfairly favoured and cosseted, but from her perspective our parents became unduly overprotective and meddling—fencing her around with restrictions about whom she could see and where she could go.

In my mind, however, we were a normal, happy family. We often played together in our expansive back garden, rode our bikes and went for walks together. On occasions we all piled into the car to go and watch a rugby seven-a-side tournament in one of the Scottish border towns or spend a day by a river or on a loch fly fishing.

During the war, Dad had evolved from being a missionary, a servant of God, to being a civil servant at the Scottish Office, based at St Andrew's House in Edinburgh. At that time I had no idea of the significance of his work, but one day my Junior School[9] teacher thrust a copy of *The Scotsman* newspaper in front of me and asked, "Is this your father?"

I quickly recognized a photo of my dad with a bold caption, "James Callan Wilson," and scanned several columns which identified him as the newly appointed accountant general of the Department of Health for Scotland. Over the ensuing years he rose through the ranks until he eventually took early retirement in order to enter the ministry of the Church of Scotland. He had clearly made a success of his civic career, but I admired him when he gave up further prospect of advancement to return to his first love. Dad and Mum were always involved in Christian ministry of some kind, both in the local church and in parachurch activities.

John's parents at his wedding (1967)

On Sunday mornings, I woke to the smell of frying sausages or bacon and eggs wafting from the kitchen. Traditionally on this day we served Mum breakfast in bed while Dad took her place at the old gas stove in the kitchen. Then, after breakfast, instead of our routine family prayers at the kitchen table, we sat around the piano

[9] George Watson's College was divided into "Prep", "Junior" and "Senior" schools.

in the drawing room and sang some favourite hymns. Without the pressure to rush out to school or work, family prayers on the Lord's Day were more relaxed, and Dad's Bible-reading and commentary were longer, more animated and sometimes even interesting.

Before leaving for church, Mum prepared the lunch and put the lamb or beef roast—never pork—into the oven. She upheld her belief that the Old Testament food laws had a foundation in practicality for good health, but evidently they were nullified when the same animal was cured as bacon. Nor did the ancient code apply to the Scottish delicacy "black pudding," which I was horrified to learn later essentially consisted of pig's blood in a length of intestine. This was quite clearly taboo according to these same dietary restrictions in the Bible, but our mother was obliviously inconsistent!

The Christianity of my parents was not merely religious "Sabbath keeping," but was grounded in the reality of daily living. While many Christians we knew were quite legalistic and rigid sabbatarians who frowned on any frivolity or sign of enjoyment on Sundays, Dad seemed to treat the day with mingled reverence and joy. I was quite surprised one summer day when, dressed in his Sunday best, he picked up a cricket bat and ball and led us out onto our expansive garden lawn to play "French cricket."[10]

---

10 In French cricket, one person stands in the middle as the batsman, protecting his legs because there are no stumps. The other players circle around the batter as fielders. Whoever retrieves the ball then tosses it back to the batter, who is out if the ball is caught or touches his legs.

In this regard, Mum was more staid, more austere and more Calvinistic and, moreover, a supporter of the Scottish Reformation Society. Generally, if there was any narrow-mindedness and legalism in my family, it came from her, and she was more likely to tell us that Christians don't do this or that. It was she who taught us Christians don't drink, don't smoke, don't dance, don't go to the movies, and—she might have added—don't have fun! However, when as a teenager I asked her why she believed some of these things, I discovered that she had a rationale founded on her reading of the Bible. It wasn't that she thought this was the way to be a "good Christian"; rather, it was that if you believed what the Bible taught, you would choose to abstain from these things.

As I look back, I see Mother as more inclined to law, while our father was more oriented to grace; she tended to be intolerant and see things as black or white, while he, on the other hand, was more lenient and magnanimous, though he could be very stern at times. Yet she, as a stay-at-home mum, was the one who was always there for us, while Dad was less involved, though not disinterested. His role in the Scottish Office meant that he often worked late, and from time to time his responsibilities took him further afield to Glasgow, or even to London. Nevertheless, I loved and respected them both.

However, there was a skeleton in the closet. While I was growing up, I never did understand the rationale, but when our parents returned to Congo after their first furlough, my oldest brother Malcolm was left in the care of our maternal grandparents.

Consequently, when the family next came home from Africa, he barely knew his parents, and more than that, he now had two strange brothers to contend with. Of course, I wasn't around to see the early dynamics of the reunited family, but by the time I was five or six years old, I was well aware of a tension between Malcolm and our parents that manifested itself in many different ways. I remember, for example, Malcolm coming home late for supper: "Why are you late again?" Mother demanded angrily. "I was at the whaler," he replied laconically. My oldest brother was active in the naval section of the cadet force at school that owned and kept the twenty-seven-foot naval craft at Leith docks. He liked to go there to potter around and do maintenance. Years later I asked him if this was just a ruse so he could go and visit a girlfriend, but his answer shocked and saddened me: "No, there wasn't a girlfriend. It was just to delay coming home. I didn't feel I was wanted."

The atmosphere was tense as Malcolm fetched the food which had been left warming under the gas grill, and as he sat down, he unwisely made a cynical observation about the dried-out and now unsavoury-looking meal. Naturally, that upset Mother even more and led to a sharp altercation. With pent-up anger and frustration, Malcolm took his knife in his clenched fist and jabbed it down hard into the china plate, which split in two, leaving the burnt offering on the table. The rest of us around the table struggled with shock and stifled laughter, not daring to say a word, while our hungry brother was dismissed supperless.

Many years later, when I was home with my parents on vacation from Bible college, I inadvertently did or said something to incur Dad's irritation. "You are just another Malcolm!" he admonished me.

My brothers and I had heard this kind of reprimand many times during our boyhood. It was a reproof with a lot of tacit baggage: Malcolm was seen as the insubordinate, rebellious son and the black sheep of the family. As the firstborn son he was supposed to be the leader and set us a good example, but his place had been unwittingly usurped by our second brother Jeff. Consequently, the corollary of this reproach was, "You need to take a leaf out of Jeffrey's book!"

To hear this oft-repeated rebuke again as a twenty-something-year-old suddenly stirred up the resentment that must have been smouldering in my heart and mind for years, and before I realized what I was doing, I challenged my dad. "Why is it that whenever you want to censure us you compare us negatively with Malcolm, but on the other hand you always hold up Jeff as the paragon of virtue? Don't you realize that a lot of Malcolm's obstinacy was a result of you leaving him at home when you went back to Africa?"

Even as I spoke, I wondered if I had overstepped the mark. I held my breath as I watched the anger and sense of offence flush in my father's face, and I waited, anticipating the inevitable explosion. But the color drained from his face, and when he spoke, his voice was choked and husky. "You are right," he said quietly. Then, after a pause he added, "That is the greatest regret of my life."

Tears welled up in his eyes as he acknowledged this fateful choice and its tragic consequences, tears I had never seen in all my years of growing up. How sad it seemed that behind his stoical outward posture beat this hurting heart, unhealed for so long! How sad that his unfortunate mistake should have remained unacknowledged and unconfessed—and unforgiven until now. How grievous that for more than thirty years the integrity and happiness of a family, and the love of a father for his son, should have been so tragically jeopardized.

That day I saw my dad in a new light. I saw him in his vulnerability—more sensitive, more humble, more approachable—and I began to understand consciously some of the tacit dynamics and tensions within our family. This single moment subtly transformed our relationship and I perceived him for the first time not so much as a father and authority figure, but as a brother, a fellow traveller in our Christian pilgrimage. It also planted within my own heart the desire for the same kind of honesty and humility he had displayed when he refused to justify himself to me, but acknowledged what to him seemed the biggest failing of his life.

What subsequently transpired between him and Malcolm is not part of my story, but I know he later wrote to my brother, who was then living in Canada, to apologize and seek a reconciliation. However, this was a watershed moment in my life. On the one hand it transformed some of the negativity which had always been there, unspoken, in our family life, and on the other, I sensed it was a landmark in my own development and self-realization. I had discerned and interpreted events and circumstances about which no one in the family had ever talked openly, but which I had found the courage (or foolhardiness) to address based on my own insight, convictions and feelings.

CHAPTER 3

A Change of Course

When I walked out through the doors of my school for the last time, it seemed to me like a rite of passage. Above the main school building, a weather vane—a gilded ship—swung in the changing wind. It represented The Company of Merchants of the City of Edinburgh, the owners and operators of this prestigious school, but perhaps it was an omen of the uncertain future I faced.

The gilded weather vane above George Watson's College

George Watson's College, which had been my scholastic habitat for thirteen years, held no graduation ceremony. Our Scottish Leaving Certificates would be mailed to our homes later, so it was this unceremonious exit which symbolized the clear break with my boyhood. Yet it meant more than that. It felt like a rude expulsion from a place of security, the place that had been home for many years. I was thrust out into the unknown world of adulthood, and I was not ready. I did not yet know who I was.

I was and still am a slow learner. I process new information slowly, and examine and analyze every fragment of data piece by piece, but I had not yet pieced together the clues about my natural gifts or aptitudes. I still had no idea what I wanted to do with the rest of my life.

On reflection, it seems to me that nobody else had a clear idea either. It had been imprinted on my mind in various ways that I wasn't academically inclined and that university should not even be considered—even though many of my peers entered a basic Arts degree program, not knowing where it would lead them. For most of my friends, that was an option that gave them the time to determine what specific course they would follow. But not me, so I sought advice.

"Wilson," the disinterested careers guidance teacher said, "Fill in this form and bring it back tomorrow." I dutifully completed the impersonal form, and before I knew it, I had applied, been interviewed, and formally apprenticed to a small Edinburgh company of chartered quantity surveyors. I was also required to enrol in a concurrent five-year-long day-release-and-night-school program at a local college.

Together with everybody else, however, I had missed the fact that there was a great deal of mathematics involved in being a quantity surveyor. Although, at Watson's, I had learned the times tables and basic arithmetic I had floundered in the mire of trigonometry and algebra, and by the time we were into logarithms and calculus, I was well over my head in the great morass called mathematics. Consequently, although I actually enjoyed some aspects of the apprenticeship, in this regard I felt like a fish out of water. What was I to do?

I had not walked into this career carelessly. While in my last year at high school, one night I had knelt alone in my bedroom to pray for guidance: "God, you know that I want to live my life for you regardless of the career pathway I follow, so please guide me in the choices I have to make."

What happened next was unexpected and beyond my ken. God came into the room. I felt his presence and I heard his voice—not in any way I could explain or you would necessarily believe, never mind understand. I am not sure if the voice was audible or extrasensory; nevertheless, I heard him speak.

"Are you willing to become a missionary?" he asked.

Knowing my family's missionary heritage, this notion was within the scope of my imagination. Maybe there was some worm of an idea deep within my unconscious, but it was certainly not at the forefront of my waking thoughts. I had assumed, as I am sure some of my brothers had done, that on leaving school I would first pursue a career, and then *perhaps* later (as our father had done) give some years to missionary service. And so I answered this intimate inquiry, "Yes, Lord, but when and where do you want me to go?"

His answer was as clear and distinct as my question: "When it is time for you to go, I will show you."

Until he showed me otherwise, then, I had blindly followed the counsel of the career guidance teacher and my parents and signed on for the five-year apprenticeship. When I later discovered it was not a natural fit for me, the thought of quitting did not cross my mind. Today, a young man wouldn't think twice about resigning and trying his hand at something else. No job nowadays is "for life"; you take your chances and live more for the moment. Conversely, in the 1960s, most people were glad to get into a career with prospects, content to knuckle under and do what it took, knowing there was job security and a good income down the road. With this in mind, I resolved to work and study hard, learn the ropes, and take my exams with a view to becoming a qualified chartered surveyor. Moreover, I was in a legally binding five-year apprenticeship.

However, in the third year of my training, something happened which unexpectedly turned my life around, setting me on a new course. With some friends, I attended a weekend missionary conference for young men and women. During that weekend, we each had to choose one of five seminars on specific countries or regions. By a process of elimination, I felt I had only one valid option. My parents had been in Congo, I knew several missionaries who had served in India, and I corresponded with a missionary in Peru, so I ended up in the seminar group that was to focus on Dutch New Guinea.

What I learned surprised and stimulated me. "Dutch New Guinea is the last unknown, a new and challenging frontier which came to the attention of the Western world in 1944," the seminar leader explained. "At that time, American troops under General McArthur's leadership landed there to oust the Japanese. During their campaign, some American planes flew sorties over the interior, and their crews observed small isolated communities scattered throughout the inhospitable mountain terrain. In fact, when one aircraft crashed near a wide, high-altitude valley surrounded by three thousand-meter-high mountain ranges, the resourceful Americans carried out a rescue mission with gliders to bring out the survivors. These airmen told remarkable stories of the Stone-Age people they encountered there."

He continued, "Soon after the war, negotiations were initiated with the Dutch government for permission to begin missionary work in these remote areas, but it wasn't until the late 1950s that the first pioneers were able to establish bases in the highland interior among a large tribe called the Dani."

I was astounded when he went on to say, "Thousands of the Dani people have been turning to Christ *en masse*, but there are dozens of other tribal groups who need to be reached with the gospel, taught to read and write, and be healed of endemic tropical diseases. The door is wide open for missionary linguists, doctors, Bible teachers and nurses."

A few days following the conference, one of my brothers and I were studying in the bedroom we shared, when suddenly he blurted out, "Why are you so restless tonight? Why can't you study quietly?"

It was only then that I realized how restive I was. I put my books aside and turned to my Bible. In my reading I had come to Acts 16, where the Holy Spirit guides Paul and his apostolic band—sometimes prompting, sometimes preventing them from going one way or another. However, when Paul tells his companions of his vision of a man begging him to cross the Aegean Sea to Macedonia, they conclude that this is God's call to them to go together and preach the gospel there. As I read and reflected on that passage it felt as if God was saying, "New Guinea is your Macedonia."

Paul's vision had been confirmed by his companions, so I resolved to test my Macedonian call with others. The first person I told was my dad, who agreed that this was a call of God on my life. However, I also had to inform my employer, who was not a Christian, nor (as far as I knew) sympathetic in any way to what I was about to say to him.

Robin Robertson, the senior partner in the firm, was a short, tight-lipped man with dark hair and dark-framed glasses. A chain smoker, with the telltale yellow stains on his fingers, he also had a sharp temper and could express his displeasure in colourful language never used in my home. After a tentative knock on the door, I heard his invitation: "Come in!"

"Sir," I began, "I would like to be formally released from the apprenticeship," and then, with some nervousness I added, "I believe God wants me to become a missionary and I plan to enter a Bible college."

His immediate response surprised me: "I cannot stand in your way if you believe that God wants you to do this." However, a few days later, when he called me back into his office, I wondered if he had had second thoughts, and I knocked on his office door with renewed trepidation.

"John, since you are the only person who has mastered the electronic calculator, I want you to teach the other apprentices before you leave."

Not only was this a monster of a machine compared to the slim handheld devices which later became commonplace, all our calculations had to be converted into decimals. Britain was only beginning to move towards decimal currency, and all our pricing was in pounds, shillings and pence. The same was the case with linear and cubic measurements, which were still in yards, feet and inches.

I was taken aback when he continued, "Also, I have decided to increase your salary so you will have some extra cash to pay for your fees when you enter the Bible training college."

Finally the day came when I left the office and quantity surveying behind me for good. One or two people had counselled me not to take this radical step. Others offered the gloomy prophecy, "You will live to regret this. When you eventually return from the mission field, John, you will need to take up your career again." It did feel as if I had burned my bridges, but there was no wavering and no turning back.

CHAPTER 4

A Door Slammed Shut

I had received a message to report to the office of "the Wee Man"—the diminutive, mild-mannered and soft-spoken, yet authoritative principal of the Bible Training Institute in Glasgow.

On the day he arrived at BTI, one of my fellow students had mistaken the white-haired Wee Man for a janitor, and had asked his help in carrying his heavy luggage up the steps into the building. Without batting an eye, he had grabbed one end of the heavy trunk and helped my friend lug it up the steps and into the foyer. However, this short, humble man also ensured that the school ran smoothly in line with its purpose, regulations and strict discipline.

While I was enjoying my biblical and theological courses, I had struggled particularly in a couple of other classes, and had already been called once to the office of "the Gentle Giant," who was introducing us to the history of philosophy of religion. This towering but soft-spoken teacher had virtually served me with an ultimatum. "Evidently, John, you are out of your depth in this class, and if you don't make significant progress next term, you will not be allowed to continue in the University of London Diploma of Theology program. Of course, you will be allowed to continue in the college's own diploma program."

I was shaken, for a moment thinking the worst. "I am confident, sir," I ventured to reply with some mental reservation, "that I will be able to do better next term. Please allow me to give it my best try." And I did! In my heart, I knew I must persevere, even with the required courses which I didn't enjoy. I was on my way to becoming a missionary, and I needed all the training I could get.

Along with some other students, I had enrolled in a theology course from the University of London which was run concurrently with the Institute's own courses. It was a challenge, not only because of the additional study load, but because there were other school requirements which made demands on our time, particularly the practical ministry assignments, which took me twice a week into a rough area of the city. Nevertheless, I pulled out the stops in the philosophy of religion class and succeeded in raising my grade to a very satisfactory level.

Now, as I knocked on the principal's door, I wondered why he had called me in.

"Come in, John, and have a seat." The kind-faced Wee Man with a backbone of steel welcomed me into his book-lined study where he sat in an old wooden desk chair beside a dark mahogany table cluttered with numerous books and papers. After some casual chitchat he continued, "I called you in for another matter, John."

"Here we go," I thought. "I'm in for a reprimand about something."

However, the Wee Man seemed to be rambling, almost talking in riddles, and having a hard job coming to the point. Eventually, it dawned on me that he was talking about another first-year student called Gloria Boatman. Here was the problem: it had come to his attention that I had "taken an interest" in Gloria.

In fact, Gloria had come to my attention at a meal table one day in the second week of school. As we stood waiting for grace to be said, I was captivated by her lovely open face, her blue-green eyes and her radiant smile—although I didn't think her French-roll hairstyle suited her. It would look far better let down around her pretty face—and that was how she appeared at the next mealtime.

However, I didn't want to be distracted by any girl so early in my time at the school because I was determined to make the most of my opportunity to study—especially so, when I began to feel the full load of my courses and assignments. Moreover, my own resolve was strengthened one day following a casual conversation with Gloria in a hallway. I asked the standard question. "What are you planning to do when you leave BTI?"

"Well, I'm interested in joining Wycliffe Bible Translators and will probably go to Brazil or somewhere else in Latin America."

That's it, then, I thought. *She's preparing to join Wycliffe and go to South America, but I'm headed in another direction, and will never be a Bible translator.* Aloud, I told her, "I'm planning to go to West Irian," and seeing the blank look on her face, clarified, "It's what used to be Dutch New Guinea."

So for the next several months, I tried to keep Gloria out of my mind, although our paths seemed to cross more and more frequently. The inevitable happened. The problem was that at BTI, if you wanted to date a girl, you were required to obtain permission from the Wee Man, and I hadn't requested it.

Quickly, I dragged my wandering attention back to what the principal was saying. "Gloria is a very fine young lady," he concluded graciously. "Let me pray for you both, and then you can go." In this way, I received the white-haired patriarch's unrequested and unanticipated blessing, and our friendship was now officially sanctioned and free to flourish.

John and Gloria at the time of their engagement

Now we were permitted to become better acquainted without furtive conversations snatched in passing. Without any embarrassment we could sit and talk together, go for walks in the streets of central Glasgow, or share a discounted meal at the *Sans Souci* just before closing time on a Saturday night.

We also played sports. On one occasion, Gloria and I were on a mixed team of first-year students in field hockey and we each scored hat tricks, leading our team to a rout of the opposition. It was fun, and we felt well-matched in more ways than one.

That summer we became engaged, and then, despite the emotional distraction, we were both able to concentrate successfully on our studies and graduate with double diplomas. Nevertheless, it seemed to me that Gloria and I were still a far cry from being ready to apply to a mission board for service. There is much more to missionary training and preparation than a few academic qualifications, but apart from that, though I'm not sure I realized it at the time, there remained in me the lurking legacy of lack of self-confidence. I needed to be more certain of myself before I could offer my life to the challenges of missionary service. We also knew that it was important to get to know each other better in the normal workaday world.

On leaving BTI, Gloria went back to her home in a north London suburb from where she commuted to work as a secretary for her former employer, an architect in the City. Meanwhile, I left Scotland for the same great metropolis, where I joined the office staff of the Regions Beyond Missionary Union (RBMU) in southwest London. My days there were filled with learning the ropes of the mission's communications department. I learned about printing, photography, audio recording and editing, and also how to write and edit mission publications.

My mentor was Ken Holmes. He was a small man, almost completely bald, with a pointed nose and rimless glasses which seemed to sharpen the penetrating, intelligent blue eyes with which he examined me. A workaholic perfectionist, he had little patience with carelessness, imperfection or incompetence, and after a couple of weeks, I felt like quitting until I realized that if I was ever to become a missionary, I needed to learn perseverance and patience—even with irascible and demanding people like him. Undoubtedly, I would have tougher challenges ahead of me.

However, it didn't take me long to get to know and respect Ken, who had been a missionary in India. Because of his wife's ill health and his son's diabetes he had been forced to return to the UK. To be working cooped up in a mission office was not his first choice, but he taught himself all the skills employed in the cause of informing and encouraging support and prayer for the mission, and in the following months he passed on to me knowledge and skills in these areas, together with some of his astute wisdom. I owe a great deal to Ken, and as our friendship grew, he shared insights and advice from his missionary experiences that later stood me in good stead.

A few months later, Gloria and I were married and moved into an attic flat which looked out onto the tops of the chestnut trees lining the west side of Wandsworth Common. We became happily and busily involved as youth leaders in a struggling Baptist church nearby, leading various activities and studies during the week. Our cramped-but-cosy little flat hosted Bible studies and became the place where the older youth and students liked to drop by at odd hours, have a meal with us, or simply hang out after church on Sunday evenings.

It was tempting to put down roots there where we had a very fulfilling and satisfying ministry in the church—also because we enjoyed our day jobs; nevertheless, we remembered our calling. About a year after our marriage, we applied to RBMU specifically with a view to being assigned to West Irian. It was going to be plain sailing, or so we thought. We had the training, we now had excellent ministry experience, and I had served a profitable year's apprenticeship with Ken Holmes in the mission office.

I was ready. We were both ready to move ahead, so we started the formal application process and duly had our medical exams and interviews. However, when the mission's board met and mulled over our application, they concluded that they could not send us to West Irian. One of their members, a medical doctor, was delegated to come and tell me that we had been turned down on health grounds.

If he had come out and said, "You are not spiritual enough," I would have wholeheartedly agreed, but to block our way on "health grounds" sounded absurd. If he had said, "John, you lack the resolute strength of character which we believe is needed in New Guinea," I couldn't have denied it. And so, I concluded that perhaps this was intended as a gentler way of dealing with someone like me with my deficiencies of temperament; a gentle letdown. In disbelief, I questioned the doctor. "You examined me personally. Did you find something specific which gave you concern about my health?"

"No, I found nothing specific, John. However, your history of asthma was the sticking point. All the members of the board were concerned about that, particularly in view of the fact that Dr. Jack Leng, who recently returned from West Irian, had suffered all the time from asthma. In fact, on his return to the UK he had to be hospitalized. The board is adamant. West Irian is no place for an asthmatic. They are not prepared to take the risk with you."

I was dumbfounded. For about four years I had been steadily heading towards becoming a missionary in West Irian, convinced that that was where God wanted me. In faith and obedience I had given up a professional career, carried a double course load at Bible school to equip myself academically, and spent over a year at the mission office learning the ropes of the home operations and so much more from Ken Holmes, and now this! I felt angry and frustrated. "Not prepared to take a risk?" I questioned. "I thought this was a 'faith' mission—doesn't that mean you trust God for *everything*, not just for the money to support you and the ministry? Did the board not recognize the call of God on my life? Isn't that the bottom-line issue, that and Christian character? Since I clearly was called by God to go to West Irian, surely a history of asthma should not be allowed to stand in my way? After all, our mission's pioneers in Congo—my own grandparents and their peers—risked health and even life when they went to Congo. Some of them even packed their goods in coffins! What has happened to our mission today that they now balk over a mere history of asthma?"

"I understand how you feel, John," the kind and youthful doctor replied. "The decision did not rest with me; it is the resolution of the board."

That night, I walked across Wandsworth Common to our attic home with a heavy and profoundly confused heart. Gloria still had to hear the news, which was really beginning to sink in.

The door had been slammed firmly shut in our faces.

CHAPTER 5

An Interlude in Isolation

The temperature had plummeted to -25° Celsius and a thick layer of hoarfrost glistened on the inside walls of our little uninsulated cottage. It was tempting to stay in bed where our body heat was maintained by a dual-control, electric over-blanket, each side dialled to the max! How thankful we were that Gloria's former boss in London had given us this as a going-away present. However, I got up and tip-toed over the cold linoleum to the bathroom where a kerosene heater had kept the pipes from freezing. Hasty ablutions over, I dressed there in the relative warmth.

We had moved from our snug attic flat with its view over the lush green of Wandsworth Common in southwest London to live just outside the remote village of Nethy Bridge, on the edge of the Grampian Mountains in the Scottish highlands. Our timber cottage stood among pine trees in a secluded corner of an old estate, which had recently been purchased for the Abernethy Outdoor Centre. I was employed as its pioneer warden. That was a grand title in this start-up phase, since I was the sole staff member and my wide-ranging duties included maintenance, bookings, and assisting with outdoor activities, as well as providing spiritual input to the youth groups who might come there.

Our immediate surroundings in the Abernethy Forest were an oasis of natural beauty and an unspoiled habitat for some seldom-seen plants, animals and birds. A botanist showed us a rare orchid behind the old coach house; pine martens and wildcats were in the area; and crossbills, long-tailed and crested tits were regular visitors to our rustic garden.

After living in the heart of a dense yet sprawling metropolis, I was delighted to be out in the wilds of Scotland where I could breathe invigorating fresh air and be revitalized by physical activities. My employer required me to take a mountain leadership-training course at nearby Glenmore Lodge, which seemed more like an outdoor-adventure holiday than anything else, and later I joined the local mountain rescue team where I picked up training in first aid and other skills.

There was opportunity for ministry too, when the local Church of Scotland minister introduced me to his colleagues, who invited me to preach in their own and in pastorless churches all over the area. One Easter Sunday I spoke at a service for skiers on the top of Cairngorm, one of the tallest peaks in the area. On another winter Sunday I was invited to preach in Scotland's highest village, Tomintoul. The route was one of the first to be closed by heavy snows, so before setting out, I had to ascertain from the local policeman if the road had been ploughed. It was a bitterly cold but beautiful, azure-sky morning as Gloria and I set out, and as we wended our way up the narrow winding road, often between snow drifts which towered over our van, we enjoyed the spectacular vistas of the Grampian Mountains.

This was a far cry from West Irian, but it was also far removed from the urban lives we were used to—especially Gloria, who was a city girl, who had never been out in lonely wild places in her life. What on earth were we doing here?

When the mission RBMU turned us down, and effectively closed the door on West Irian, we had wondered and prayed about what to do. It was tempting to stay in London where we had a comfortable life leading the flourishing youth group, and where I was also given regular preaching engagements with the South London Baptist Lay Preachers' Association. But we also sensed that Wandsworth was not where we should stay and put down roots.

One of the opportunities that opened up to us was the challenge to help get Scotland's first Christian outdoor-activities centre up and running. We were put in touch with a visionary Christian businessman, Norman Walker, who had formed the Abernethy Trust and funded the purchase of Abernethy House with its spacious lands outside the village of Nethy Bridge. He was looking for someone suitable to become the warden.

At that time, I was bewildered by the closing of the door on West Irian, and filled with deep disappointment and the sense of rejection that decision had brought into my life. I felt glad to seize this opportunity and to put some distance between me and the mission, so I accepted the invitation. With Gloria I packed a van and left for this new venture in Scotland.

Coming to live in this isolated spot in the Scottish highlands, working with my hands and attending to the maintenance of the grounds and facilities kept me occupied, but it also gave me ample solitude for reflection. For a while, I continued to mull over and over in my heart the signs and steps which had led me ultimately to London and the resolve Gloria and I shared to apply to be missionaries. Again and again I had wondered about the rationale of the mission board's decision, and inevitably doubts arose in my mind about the stated health issue. There had to be more to their decision than that. Surely the board had their reservations about my spiritual maturity and my character?

It was true that, as a boy, I had put up with quite severe asthma, but I had not allowed it to stop me from swimming, playing rugby, hiking, canoeing, camping and other physical activities. *Look at me now*, I thought. *I'm working hard in the outdoors every day, I can carry a thirty-kilogram pack up a mountain and still pass others on the way, I'm skinny, but wiry and strong. In short, I'm healthy*."

Day by day Gloria and I prayed for God's direction in our lives. We still felt sure we had not been mistaken about the call to serve him in West Irian, and we began to wonder whether the door was in fact permanently shut. So in the end we wrote a brief letter to Ernest Oliver, the executive director of the mission, asking simply, "Will the RBMU board be willing to consider a fresh application from us with a view to going to West Irian?"

Sometime soon afterwards, the local postman arrived in his little red Royal Mail van and handed me two distinctively flimsy blue airmail letters. I remember the day clearly. The sun was shining and as I stood chatting with the mailman, a tiny little goldcrest suddenly alighted on the red van right beside us. For a moment, we were frozen in time, our conversation interrupted, as we both stood motionless, enjoying this unexpected and unusual sight. Just as suddenly it took off, and we also parted.

It turned out that the two letters came from missionaries in West Irian: one from a friend, a medical doctor, and the other from a total stranger. Our doctor friend Liz Cousens wrote, "I think you should reapply to RBMU, because I don't see any reason asthma should prevent you from working here. With modern medications, we can keep it under control."

The second came from Costas Macris, a Greek missionary whom we had never met. He encouraged us, "If you believe God has called you here, ask the RBMU board in London to reconsider your application, and if they turn down your request, write and apply through the USA or Canadian board!" Costas—as we got to know him later—was not the kind of man to stop at any obstacle.

Before we could even acknowledge those two letters, we received a response from Ernest Oliver in London, written in his flowing, trademark calligraphy. "It is not necessary to reapply," he wrote. "And the board will reconsider your application; nonetheless, you, John, will be required to have a thorough medical examination, which we will arrange for you with a specialist in Glasgow."

On the appointed day, Gloria and I made the trip by road from our isolated little home in the heart of the highlands to a doctor's office in the heart of the grimy city of Glasgow. Over the course of several hours, I was prodded and probed and subjected to an array of rigorous tests: a chest x-ray, blood tests and an electrocardiogram. At the end of all this, the physician declared, "I see no medical cause to prevent you from going as a missionary to West Irian. In fact," he added, "I wouldn't be surprised if you are a lot fitter than some of the missionaries already there!"

We felt vindicated, and presumed it would be only a matter of months before we would be on our way to the opposite end of the earth. However, we were learning that, in God's calendar for us, time hastened slowly. We knew that we had to apply for Indonesian visas, which at the best of times can be a slow and tedious process, and we learned that no visas for West Irian had been granted for months. Obviously we could be waiting for a long time yet, so there was no point resigning from my job or thinking about packing our belongings.

Too late! My employer, Norman Walker, obviously was not on the same calendar. When he learned that we had been accepted by RBMU, fearful that we would suddenly up and leave the outdoor centre in the lurch, he immediately asked me to resign. It was fair enough, since he thought we might leave at any moment, and he wanted to be able to recruit and appoint a new warden before the start of the busy spring season. However, it was just before Christmas. Unexpectedly jobless and homeless, and, to complicate matters, with Gloria six months pregnant, we moved in temporarily with my parents, who at that time lived at Fintry in Stirlingshire.

Fortunately, my dad had learned that the Church of Scotland's Home Missions department was looking for young men to serve as lay missionaries in remote parishes in the highlands and islands, and put a word in the ear of the right person. The fact that I was a Baptist apparently didn't deter the staunch Presbyterian head of the department, who simply remarked to my father, "I don't mind if he's a Baptist as long as he preaches the gospel."

Within a few weeks, I was employed and installed in a century-old, whitewashed stone manse in Arinagour village on the Isle of Coll, one of the Inner Hebrides on the west of Scotland. The house stood alone at the end of the village street, enclosed by a drystone wall which the sheep were in the habit of jumping with remarkable ease, a mere stone's throw from the sea at high tide. The wee stone kirk where I was to minister had a commanding, bleak position on a hill outside the village overlooking the bay.

Arinagour, the Isle of Coll, from the kirk. The white manse stands at the end of the village (photo Phil Seale)

This small, low-lying, wind-swept and basically treeless island was then home to a population of 133, which included several memorable characters I got to know as I met them going about their daily lives or when I visited them in their scattered homes around the island and in the village of Arinagour.

Since Coll is less than twenty-five kilometers long and five wide, it didn't take me long to get around on the narrow road that ran almost from end to end and connected with the village. And although some of the crofts and farms were off the one-and-only road, I enjoyed hiking across the moors or along the shores to reach these places and get to know the people.

There were Iain the Post, who manned the little wooden shack called the post office; Callum the Post, who delivered the mail around the island in his little red mail van; Hughie Handy and Iain the Road, who maintained the island's few miles of single-track road; Big Archie, a retired policeman with one bad eye, but possessed of (so they said) "the second sight"; the shy and reclusive bachelor twins Hector and Archie, who scraped out a living on a tiny croft at Sorisdale on the northern tip of Coll; and Neilly John, the alcoholic lobster fisherman who artfully manoeuvred his little clinker boat among the rocks and tides. These and others soon made us feel welcome, helped by my status in their eyes as "the meenister," yet keeping the respectful distance dictated by their native shyness and reserve towards outsiders.

Annie Achamore was a spinster living alone in an isolated farmhouse. Achamore was the name of the farm, not her surname, and Annie reminded me of Pip's benefactor in *Great Expectations*. However, my Miss Havisham had not been jilted, although she had been prohibited by her parents from marrying her sweetheart because he belonged to the wrong church. Instead of a fading wedding dress, she wore layers of moth-eaten woollen clothes enclosed in a wraparound burlap sack secured with binder twine. There was no decaying cake on her table, but there were dry scraps of old meals. And in a dingy alcove of her drafty, cobweb-draped kitchen was her bed. Like many others I visited in their homes, she always offered me a *strupach,* or as they quaintly put it in English, "a cup of tea in the hand."

While it was allowable for me to call each of these fascinating people by their nicknames, it was a mark of respect that professionals be addressed correctly by title and surname, or referred to as the doctor, the nurse, and the schoolteacher. So I became "the meenister" and was addressed formally as "Mr. Weelson."

Gloria didn't join me immediately, since she was expecting our first baby and there was no hospital on the island. Normal transport to and from Coll was by MacBrayne's ferry out of Oban, which plied between the islands of the Inner Hebrides three times a week. In medical emergencies—weather permitting—a small twin-engined aircraft could land on a short grass strip to take patients to Glasgow. Otherwise, the only way on and off the island was by sea.

The Isle of Coll was blessed with a well-qualified and competent doctor whose wife was the midwife. Dr. Gaius Sutton had taken this lonely posting because he was fed up with his busy urban practice in Bristol, but also because he loved the sea, the outdoors and a slower pace of life. However, because of the remoteness of Coll and the fact that this was her first pregnancy, Dr. Sutton had advised me to have Gloria remain on the mainland to have her baby prior to coming.

I was fortunate that the date of our son Jonathan's arrival coincided with a day that the ferry returned to Oban on the mainland, so I made the crossing and then hitched a ride south. I was able to go straight to the hospital in Stirling—not far from the memorial to William Wallace of *Braveheart* fame—to see Gloria with our firstborn. A few days later, I returned to Coll with my family. That day, the island's population reached 136.

If Nethy Bridge had seemed remote and isolated to my city-born English wife, island life felt like a world even further removed. At the time, I don't think I appreciated how much the loneliness and isolation affected her, though it was mitigated by the open-heartedness and kindness of the Coll natives and a few outsiders who befriended us.

Unexpectedly, shy Effie Maclennan became one of those people. Effie lived with her children in a small, secluded croft by the shore at Caolis an Eilean, only accessible by walking along the rocky coastline from the Arinagour pier. One day when she came to visit at the manse, she was horrified to find Gloria down on her knees washing the wooden floors. "Surely the meenister's wife should not be doing the chores!" she exclaimed. "They should be giving you someone to help in the home." Gloria insisted that she didn't mind doing it and didn't need anyone to help her, but invited Effie to join her for the first of many future *strupachs* of tea over the following months.

At the other end of the social scale was a wealthy gentleman known simply as "the Dutchman." Jan de Vries, who had purchased half the island from the incumbent Laird for a personal agricultural project and holiday home, saw fit to assume some of the "lairdly" obligations to visit the lowlier folk on his land. It was not unusual for him or his wife to bestow some tangible kindness on them, perhaps some baked Dutch goodies or a freshly shot brace of pheasants, and we were included.

On one occasion, he wondered how, since we were not whisky drinkers, we managed to keep out the winter's damp cold in the drafty old manse. I don't remember what we said to that, but not long afterwards his green Land Rover came by and his game-keeper delivered a propane-gas room heater, with the word that when the bottle of gas ran out, we were just to let him know and he would refill or replace it at no cost to us.

Coll had a culture of its own, and most of its native inhabitants had "the Gaelic" as their first language, so we look back on our time there as our first truly cross-cultural experience. We had to learn their ways and idiosyncrasies, and if we had planned to remain there permanently and become genuinely accepted, we would have had to learn to speak "the Gaelic." Besides that, the pace and manner of life was different to anything we had known. Clocks and calendars were not as important as tides, gale warnings and the schedule for the ferry. There was no electric light, except at the doctor's house and the "hotel" (which was more like the local pub), where there were diesel generators. Instead, everyone else managed with kerosene or "Calor" gas lamps. There were phones, but only one shared line to the mainland, so you had to listen to see if anyone else was on and take care not to say anything private that you didn't want broadcast around the island.

And news travelled fast there, one way or another. By phone call, by word of mouth in the shop and the post office, to every passing motorist on the road, and by Callum the post as he went his rounds in the red Royal Mail van. I remember one day when our phone rang. It was the pier master: "Hello, Mr. Weelson. Some strangers just disembarked from the boat, and seemingly they are Jehovah's Witnesses." The adverb "seemingly" was a guarded caveat when passing on some juicy gossip. Then he added, "I have also told Mr. McLeod at the Free Kirk manse, so you will be letting your flocks know."

Mr. McLeod, like myself, was a lay missionary from the other Presbyterian kirk on Coll, and it was unquestioningly accepted that we would pass the word along to everyone on the island not to welcome these folk into their homes and not even to give them a *strupach.* Thus the unfortunate visitors had a cool reception wherever they went around the island, and were glad to find refuge at the hotel until the MacBrayne's ferry came in two days time.

Eventually, our time on Coll came to an end. There was hopeful news about the processing of our visa for Indonesia. So the day came for us to leave the island, with kind farewells from many of the locals who came to the pier to see us off. After crossing by ferry to the Scottish mainland, we were to head south to London to prepare a shipment of essential household goods, tools and clothing, and otherwise prepare to fly halfway around the world to an even more remote place—what had been called "the last unknown" and by this time was called Irian Jaya.

Our temporary stay on the island of Coll while we were waiting had drawn out to a year and a half, but it had been worthwhile and enjoyable. We felt that our cross-cultural encounter with the "Collachs"—as they are called in Gaelic—had been good training for us, not to mention the ministry experience, the different pace of life, the isolation, and the lack of many of the modern amenities and conveniences of the city. It had not been an interruption, but a preparatory interlude in our journey.

PART 2

PAPUA (1971-1991)

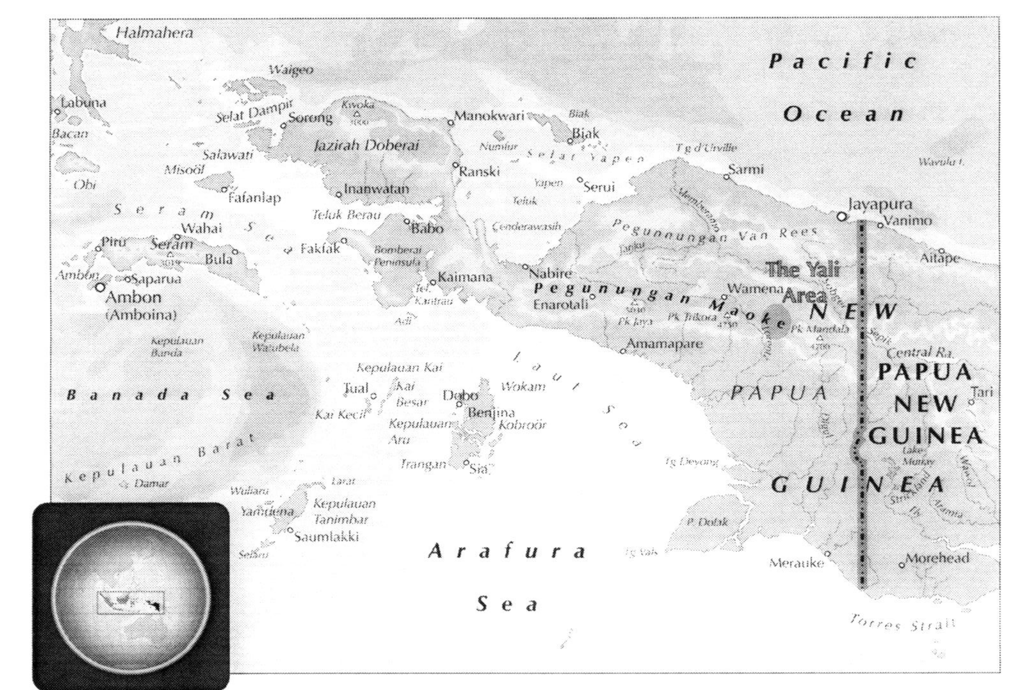

Map of Papua, Indonesia (Drawn by Mark Porter for John Wilson)

CHAPTER 6

Cannibals at Christmas

Morning sunlight slants through the narrow doorway, creating a swirling paisley-patterned hologram in blue smoke from the smouldering fire. The wooden, windowless hut is round. Its occupants, all men, squat on their haunches or sit cross-legged around the central fireplace, their conversation a quiet murmur. One man smokes a rolled leaf of tobacco, another seems lost in his own world, as he quietly evokes a rhythmic thrum from his bamboo mouth harp, and a third is engrossed in carving a barbed hardwood arrowhead with piece of pig tusk. A native dog, looking half dingo and half African Basenji, its foreleg hobbled with a strip of vine, hops agilely out through the narrow doorway, while another lies curled peacefully at his master's feet. The rising smoke forms a dense layer above their heads as it seeks a way upward through the low, tar-blackened bamboo ceiling into the overhead, sleeping platform, eventually to seep through the unseen thatch above or escape through chinks in the walls under the eaves.

Outside, the night's chill still pervades the mountain air, so the smoke filtering through the leaf thatch of the cluster of two dozen huts hangs momentarily in a hazy pall above the village. Soon it begins to drift slowly downhill, where for a few moments it is caught among the trees like cobwebs until dissipated by the warming sun as it rises higher above the eastern mountains.

Two young girls stand on a rock to warm themselves in the sunshine, hugging themselves against the cold, arms crossed over their chests and hands clasped behind their necks. A woman emerges from a small hut and scurries across the village yard, carrying a net bag of freshly baked sweet potatoes to the dominant men's hut, where she passes it through the doorway to unseen hands. A pig squeals and grunts contentedly to be released from its pen in a woman's hut into the confines of a small fenced yard. An unfed baby cries lustily for its mother's breast and a little boy shares his hot sweet potato with a fussing hen and her peeping chicks. A wiry, bearded man—stone axe hooked over his shoulder, bow and arrows in hand, and hunting dog at his heels—picks his way between muddy puddles on the path leading from the village. Soon others will follow: men will set off to the forest to collect bark, vine and other materials for building, or to clear an area of forest to make a new vegetable garden. Women and girls—often with infants on their shoulders or in a string bag on their backs—will head to the cultivated slopes to plant, weed and harvest sweet potatoes, yams, taro and traditional leafy crops.

A typical Yali village at dawn

This idyllic scene had been repeated daily with little variation for countless generations in the steep-sided valleys of Papua's mountainous, isolated interior.

Nevertheless, the seemingly pacific life of these mountain horticulturalists was not free from danger, disease and death.

Earthquakes and landslides caused devastation and disaster in seconds, tearing a garden and all its produce from its precarious hold on the mountain or engulfing a village in a tide of mud and rocks. The periodic visit of El Niño-disrupted weather brought drought, an unusually prolonged wet season caused crops to rot in the saturated soil and hindered fresh planting, or a rare but ruinous sweet-potato blight stunted growth and reduced the crop. Each resulted in a perilous food shortage and hunger, which was stoically endured as a fact of life.

Unpredictable epidemics of influenza regularly afflicted the villagers, periodic plagues of dysentery swept with amazing rapidity through the community, and endemic malaria regularly took its toll. Life expectancy was low, infant mortality high. A man might take two wives and see twenty or more children born, but in his old age be survived by only one or two sons.

Moreover, there was intratribal hostility. Villages on one side of the valley allied themselves against those on the other to exact revenge for long-past as well as recent offences of theft or killing. Who knew when or why the cycle of conflict had started? Perhaps some hot-blooded youth, supported by his peers, had raped or abducted a young girl and men had been killed in the attempt to avenge the rape or rescue the girl. Inevitably, a sequence of revenge and payback killings had ensued as they tried to settle the score. This ceaseless cycle of vengeance had gone on for generations, fostered by the making of fetishes for slain family members to invoke the spirits and summon the strength and prowess of ancestors to aid the warriors. Attacks were ruthless and undiscriminating, against men and women, old and young, and sometimes ended in the cannibalization of the victim in taunting sight of the enemy.

The irony was that, according to ancestral lore, Yali enemies could trace their joint lineage back through seven generations to the same primal ancestors. A young Yali man who refused to participate in a vindictive cannibal feast later confessed to me, "All I could think was that these were my own flesh and blood."

These were the people among whom Gloria and I had come to live, in a village called Ninia. When we arrived there in 1972, we had immediately immersed ourselves in learning the Yali language and trying to understand their culture. Now it was already our second Christmas in Papua.[11]

A young man called Yariut who was helping us in the kitchen ran his thumb along the blade of a freshly sharpened knife while he recounted how he had once participated in a cunning ambush followed by a cannibal feast in his home village.

The Yali population was not dense, but mostly clustered in small scattered hamlets and villages on hilltops or ridges, with adjacent clearings for their sweet-potato gardens on the steep slopes below. Villages were widely separated by rushing rivers, rugged mountain outcrops, and vast tracts of unspoiled rainforest.

---

11 We arrived in Papua in 1971, and spent several months of orientation among the Dani people in Karubaga in the Swart Valley. We moved to live among the Yali in Ninia in July 1972.

I had already been to Yariut's village, an arduous day's hike to the south. As I listened to him, I could picture the round, thatched huts strung out like a row of brown mushrooms along a mountain ridge, from where the villagers had a commanding view across the deep valley towards the area inhabited by their traditional enemies, the Baiye. Their common boundary was the thundering brown width of the thrusting Balim River far below as it threaded its tortuous way through the mountains to the lowlands.

"Our elders had sent messengers across the valley," Yariut began, still testing the knife's edge with his thumb. "They had been told to say, 'Come and bring pigs for barter to the confluence of the Heluk and Balim Rivers. We have recently traded with the villages of Oukele and Uwam towards the south and we have brought back many powerful, black-palm bows. We know you prize these highly, so get your pigs together, and we for our part will build a new bridge. When the new moon appears, watch for a smoke signal to say that all is ready.'"

"With this ruse," Yariut chuckled, "our men planned an ingenious ambush. First, we constructed a new bridge where the Balim and Heluk Rivers come together. Beside the bridging point there is a small flat clearing where the trade was to take place.

"However, we had constructed the bridge in such a way that when the Baiye men crossed over carrying the pigs, our men would be able, with a few swift axe cuts to strategic vines, to collapse the entire bridge behind them into the raging torrent below.

"Early on the appointed day, some of us hid in the bush with our weapons, our hearts pulsating with nervous anticipation, while others stood unarmed in the open with the bows and arrows for trade lying in bundles on the ground. As the morning sun's rays penetrated the deep valley, Baiye men appeared on the far side of the river, but before they crossed, cautious words of greeting and readiness to trade were shouted back and forth above the roaring of the river. With those assurances, the traders started out across the bridge, bearing squealing pigs, feet in the air, on their shoulders. One by one, they arrived on our side of the river." We listened, riveted, feeling the tension mount as Yariut told the story.

"But suddenly they smelt us. Those of us hiding in the bush were perspiring in the heat and excitement," he explained. "When they caught the whiff of our body odour and started to run, we erupted from our hiding places, brandishing machetes and axes to cut the bridge loose and attack the startled Baiye traders. Some of them succeeded in getting onto the bridge before it collapsed into the rushing river. A handful—one with his arm severed by an axe-blow—escaped to the other side. However, those who had already moved into the clearing couldn't escape. We felled them with a hail of arrows fired into their bodies at close range."

Heedless of our unrestrained gasps, he went on. "In full sight of the Baiye escapees on the other side of the river, some of our men proceeded to butcher the hapless victims. While the butchering was going on, we rounded up the pigs, who had scattered, and gathered the bundles of untraded bows and arrows. Meanwhile, the older men wrapped the body parts in leaves and distributed them among the ambush party. I was given a leg to shoulder and bring back up the mountain to our village."

We listened, speechless, but held hostage to this horrifying insight into Yali custom, into an event which had happened during the lifetime of this teenaged storyteller. Cannibalism was a merciless taunt, even more so after such a cruel betrayal as on this occasion, only a couple of years before we arrived at Ninia.

Yariut's story was a salutary reminder that behind the dramatic beauty of the landscape and the idyllic scenes of daily village life we had observed lay the grim realities of fear of spirits and enemies, cruel and irrational customs, and of course the ever-present sickness, suffering and premature death.

It also reminded us that most of the Yali people had yet to hear the gospel. In and around Ninia, the mission post opened by Stan Dale, there were perhaps by this time a couple hundred believers and hundreds more inquisitive folk who regularly attended the teaching meetings in their villages. But further afield, to the south and east, there were thousands who had not yet heard the gospel message, let alone come to faith in Christ. That was why we had come—but how were we to accomplish this? How soon would Christ be born in their hearts?

CHAPTER 7

Learning to Speak

"What do you dread most about going to West Irian?"

A Yali man greets John in the traditional way

That was one question people often posed when they learned that we were going to serve as missionaries in what is now called Papua. Their *first* question was usually, "Where in the world is that place?" On one occasion, a person prayed for "John and Gloria Wilson who are on their way to West Ham"—a neighbourhood in east London, traditionally known for its football team. And on another occasion, they had us on our way to west Iran! However, once they had figured out that it was the western part of New Guinea, that great dinosaur of an island perched to the north of Australia—"the land that time forgot" inhabited by "stone-age cannibals"—then their *next* questions were about fear.

"Aren't you scared to go to such a remote and primitive place?"

"Don't you worry about tropical diseases like malaria and dysentery?"

"Aren't you afraid to take your little boy to live among cannibals?"

It is true that what usually causes fear is the unknown, the unpredictable and the uncontrollable, so naturally we had some apprehensions about all those things. And you can be sure we talked to people who had been to New Guinea, and read everything about the place that we could. However, one time I confessed, "What I fear most is that we will have to learn an unwritten tribal language. I hear the languages are very difficult, and if I fail to master the local lingo, what good will I be?"

That was what I really dreaded, deep down in my heart; that I would be an abject failure as a missionary. I imagined the humiliation of not making the grade and the possibility that we would have to return home to face family and friends in shame and disgrace. My old nemesis—lack of confidence in my ability and fear of failure—had come to haunt me again. So when the mission allocated us to Ninia, I was encouraged to know that we would have a seasoned and experienced missionary, Bruno de Leeuw, as our teacher and mentor.

Gloria and I were delighted when Bruno told us, "I will teach you everything I know about the language." We began to meet with him every morning, usually with a Yali beside us to guide our pronunciation, but ten lessons later, he informed us, "I have taught you everything I know!"

I had assumed Bruno was fluent in the Yali language already. As a single man, he had helped the Australian missionary Stan Dale begin the work at Ninia, but he subsequently lived and worked among the Dani people, and from all accounts was fairly competent in *their* language. However, when Stan was killed by the Yalis in 1968, Bruno and his wife Marlys were asked to move to Ninia, and when we arrived, they had only been there permanently about a year and a half. Suddenly it dawned on us: Bruno was still learning the Yali language. And, sad to say, there were no notes available from Stan Dale, who, from what the Yali people told us, had learned the language well.

Nevertheless, we had much to learn from Bruno—a humble, godly man of prayer and a determined and courageous pioneering missionary. One day, soon after we arrived at Ninia, Bruno took me aside. "John," he said, "If you see me doing anything you question, please tell me. If what I am doing is wrong, I need to be corrected; if I am right, you need to understand why."

The humility and wisdom of this good-humoured, winsome Dutchman was irresistible, and I entered into a warm comradeship and fellowship with him. I found him to be a great mentor in the practical as well as the spiritual dimensions of missionary life. As far as the language was concerned, though, we were now on our own.

But here was the rub! We didn't have linguistic training, so how were we to go about learning this language? Back in England Gloria and I had once asked the mission director, "Is it necessary for us to take a course at the Summer Institute of Linguistics before going to Irian Jaya?"

"No," he had replied emphatically. "There are several linguists who have been working there and they have already analyzed the language, put it into written form, and made language notes." The problem, however, was that there are more than 250 languages in the province of Papua, and while it was true that linguists had completed the analysis of a few of them, many more still remained unexamined and unwritten.

Initially, any strange language sounds like an aimless jumble of indistinguishable sounds and syllables, and I remember wondering, "How can I ever learn Yali without the aid of grammar notes or a dictionary?"

When Yali people spoke among themselves, it sounded like a combination of the glug-glug of water poured from a bottle, punctuated with incessant throat-clearing and rolling r's. Now, as a Scot, I can roll my r's, and I knew that I would be able to get fairly close to those guttural sounds, but as my ears became better attuned and the Yalis began to teach me individual words, I also became aware that they had several specific sounds in their language which were unlike anything in my Scottish speech. Part of the challenge of learning Yali was to find out how to articulate these new sounds. In fact, even before trying to pronounce them, I had to learn to "hear" them; I needed to be able to distinguish, for example, between a "k" sound made at the front of the mouth and another made at the back of the mouth.

The expression "tongue twister" really does describe what I sometimes had to do. I had to train my tongue to do things it had never done before—to arch or curl it in order to touch parts of my mouth it had not been used to touching. Or, I had to make unfamiliar shapes with my mouth to form vowels that were quite different from my own.

I developed a daily language-learning routine, a combination of fieldwork and deskwork. Without a grammar or dictionary, I first had to gather and compile information to study: word lists, phrases and verbs. I followed Bruno's advice and carried a small notebook in my pocket so I could jot down the new words and phrases I overheard or elicited as I walked around the nearby villages and the valley, observing people going about their daily tasks.

I had asked Bruno to help me learn some questions, and armed with these, I asked, "What is the name of that?" or "What are you doing?" There was always a response, often with more information than I could understand, but whatever the answer, I jotted it down in my handy notebook for later review and analysis.

A young Yali man called Omalum volunteered to help me learn his language, and each afternoon when he came to the house, we went through my notes and he would attempt to correct my pronunciation. "This is how you say it," he'd explain, repeating the word and showing me how he formed it in his mouth. If possible, he would clarify the meanings and teach me other sentences with the same words.

With Omalum's help, I made steady progress. Most of the time it seemed very slow, but eventually a day would come when a number of pieces would quite suddenly come together. When that happened it was exciting and heartening to make a leap forward.

"Everyone is praying for you," he said encouragingly. "We believe God sent you to us to teach us his Word, so he will help you learn our words." I did learn words—lots of them. But it takes more than memorized vocabulary to be able to speak meaningful sentences. I also had to master the complicated system of verb forms and learn how to construct and speak understandable sentences. I could see light at the end of this formidable tunnel, but real fluency would come only when I could speak without thinking consciously about what I wanted to say. In the first months, that day seemed a long way off.

Nevertheless, the more I immersed myself in the study of the language the more I enjoyed it. Language analysis seemed to me like detective work or doing a fascinating jigsaw puzzle. The words and phrases in my notebook now had identifiable shapes, colours, and nuances, and I began to realize how they could be connected to each other—nouns, adjectives, adverbs, verbs and conjunctions—to make intelligible phrases, sentences and even conversations!

The verbs were a particular puzzle. Each one seemed like a sentence in itself, compressed into one convenient zip file. The verb had its root meaning like "to tell" or "to give," to which you could add suffixes that identified who was doing the telling, to whom, and when. Like the Latin and French I had studied at school, Yali verbs didn't all work the same way; they had different forms of conjugation. Eventually, I figured out that there were thirteen classes of verbs, with three past tenses, two future tenses, a present tense, several imperative forms, a subjunctive mood, and an amazing assortment of subtle compound forms.

One day Bruno and I were hiking to some villages south of Ninia when the men who were with us pointed out where the two Yali men, Yeikwaroho and Bingguok, had been ambushed and martyred while on the first evangelistic outreach from Ninia. As they told us the story, one of them used the subjunctive form: "If Yeikwaroho had gone that way, he would have escaped, but he went up the river and so he was trapped when he came to the waterfall."

My ears pricked up. This was the subjunctive form I was searching for! Now I knew how to say that verse in the story of Lazarus where Martha says to Jesus, "If you had been here, my brother would not have died." I immediately tried it out as we hiked up the mountain with our Yali companions. "If you had been with them, what would you have done?" They caught my excitement at understanding this and helped me as I tried out other similar sentences like, "If they had not volunteered to come here, they would not have died that day." Learning a language this way was better than being in a sterile language lab.

Bruno overheard my conversation and with typical humility commented, "John, I see you are going to overtake me in the language, and I look forward to you teaching me what you learn!" In time his prediction was realized, and within eighteen months, with Bruno's gracious encouragement, I preached my first message in Yali. I pretty much had to write it all out and read most of it, but I was beginning to get a handle on the language.

Twenty years later, I met a young man who was a stranger to me. "Where are you from?" I asked.

"I'm from Banga, in the Solo Valley."

"I've been there," I told him, "but you must have been a boy the first time I walked to Banga."

"That's true, my father. I was a boy about so high," he said, indicating with his hand. "But I remember that day and I still remember the words you spoke. You told us about the man who went out to sow seed, but as he scattered the seed it fell on different kinds of soil. You said the seed was the gospel, and the different soils represent the hearts of different kinds of people. I was only a boy, but I understood and remembered what you said." In that way, I learned that my first-ever message in Yali had been understood.

My confidence in the language continued to grow, and I began to think about translating some Bible passages for teaching. There wasn't much of the Scripture available yet in the Yali language. Stan Dale had made a provisional translation of the gospel of Mark, and Bruno had made simple translations of other portions which I had begun to study initially as a language-learning exercise. But with my growing understanding of Yali grammar and vocabulary, I began to see the need for corrections and more precise and idiomatic ways to translate some words and phrases. It was clear that if I was going to preach and teach, we needed to get more of the Scriptures translated. I wasn't trained for translation, so the question was, "Who will do it?"

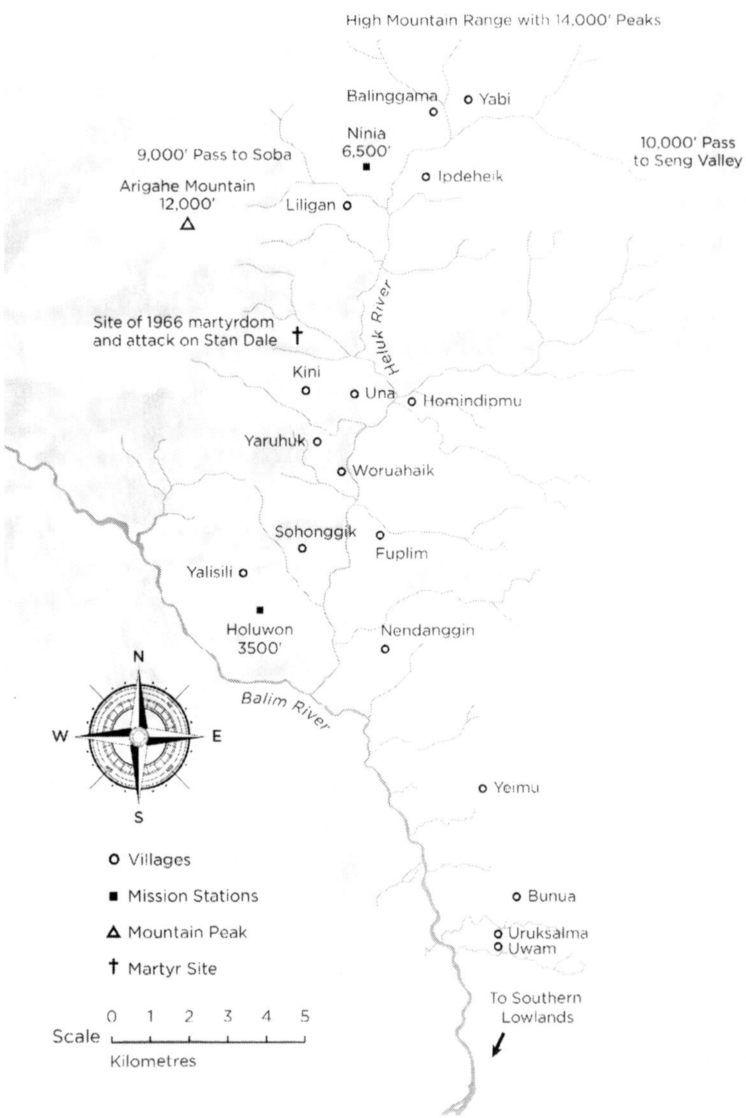

Map of the Heluk Valley (drawn by Mark Porter for John Wilson)

CHAPTER 8

Heavy-Heart Hill

During this time, unknown to me, a sequence of events had been set in motion that was to have a profound impact on my life. At the southern end of the Heluk River Valley there was a cluster of villages where the gospel was just beginning to be planted, but there was some resistance—particularly in a lonely village called Nendanggin. This small, seemingly insignificant village of about 120 people had a sad history.

At daybreak one day, a party of warriors from Uwam—a Yali community a day's journey further to the south—had conducted a vengeful raid on a village called Yeimu. With blood-curdling yells and harsh curses, a swarm of armed and angry men drove out the villagers, men, women and children. They stole their pigs, set fire to a number of huts, tore up tobacco plants, sweet potatoes, yams and taro from garden plots around the village, and hacked down a grove of precious sago palms. Remarkably, no one was killed in this devastating attack, but the Yeimu villagers had to flee northwest through the forest to start a brand new settlement on a prominent but isolated knoll, an outcrop of limestone surrounded by virgin rainforest.

They called it Nendanggin, which meant "My heart is heavy," a poignant expression of how the villagers must have felt that day. They had been driven by their enemies from their home, their land and their food supply, and were forced to start life over again in this desolate spot. It was fortunate for them that not all their sweet-potato gardens were destroyed, and that in the ensuing months the men were able to sneak back at dawn or dusk to harvest the remaining crops while establishing new garden plots nearer to the new village. At this altitude, 1500 meters above sea level, sweet potatoes—the staple—would take fewer than six months from planting to maturity. In addition, they could hunt and scavenge in the surrounding forest to augment their sparse diet with herbs, roots, nuts and bananas, and the occasional bird, marsupial, wild boar or cassowary.[12]

One day two women were returning through the forest to Nendanggin. With hand-woven net bags loaded with garden produce hoisted on their backs, they trudged barefoot and head-down as they wended their weary way along the muddy forest floor. As they walked, their eyes shifted constantly, taking in their surroundings, noting the familiar landmarks—a large *batie* oak tree, a clump of *bohweap* bamboo, the creek running crystal

[12] The cassowary is a large flightless bird, native to New Guinea and parts of Northern Australia.

clear over calcium-encrusted rocks called *fembu*—always wary of the possibility of enemy attack. Suddenly, out of the corner of her eye, one of them noticed something in the forest. "Look!" she exclaimed excitedly to her companion, "There's a new cassowary nest!"

Dropping their heavy loads, they dug enthusiastically with their hands in the pile of decomposing leaves and humus on the forest floor where this large flightless bird had laid its eggs to incubate. "I've found them," one of them exclaimed, as she extracted two giant green eggs, each weighing about half a kilogram, and each about the equivalent volume of eight chicken eggs. The women carefully wrapped the treasure in fresh leaves and ferns and placed them gently on top of the vegetables in one of their net bags.

Continuing their homeward journey, climbing steadily through the forest, they gradually became aware of a movement to the side. Their alert ears and sharp eyes detected a cassowary strutting along through the trees parallel to them, cocking its beady eye in their direction. Though this was unusual—the bird would normally run away from human contact—they didn't give it any thought. But when they got home they found that one of the eggs had exploded inside the leaf bundle.

Some villagers solemnly pronounced, "This is a sinister omen." Nevertheless, that night, two hungry families enjoyed a generous treat of scrambled eggs baked on a hot stone, while the women recounted how and where they had found the eggs, and how the cassowary had walked alongside them for some minutes through the forest.

Within a few days, first one and then the other of these two mothers took ill and died soon afterwards. Now there were no doubts. Everyone in the village remembered what the two women had said about the flightless bird's strange behaviour and the exploded egg. The cassowary had seen and resented the plundering of its nest and now its spirit had taken revenge.

By this time, however, the sickness that had taken the lives of the two hapless women had become an epidemic in the village. One after another, people fell ill, and several died. The medicine men consulted with each other and employed their esoteric arts of divination in order to ascertain how they might placate the spirits, allay the effects and halt the spread of this sickness.

"Such a severe plague indicates that it wasn't just the cassowary spirit who was displeased," one of the men boldly asserted. "Clearly other spirits too are angry."

Another added, "Our ancestral spirits must be displeased because the sacred fetishes and ancestral objects have been destroyed by those who want to listen to and follow the new message the white men and their helpers have brought."

"The only way to stop the sickness and placate the spirits is to stop these people and anyone who spreads the message from coming here," suggested another.

"*Demdoho abi!* That's true," one of his companions confirmed. "We must remake our revenge fetishes in the name of our ancestors. Only then will their spirits be placated."

Meanwhile, far up the valley at Ninia, I was oblivious to this unfolding drama. One morning, I rose early to read my Bible and pray. It was my habit to sit by a window where I could look out across the valley. Immediately below our little timber house was a row of wispy casuarina trees—so named because the drooping branches carry whorls of tiny leaves that look like the feathers of the cassowary bird—and I watched for a moment as some small colourful flower-peckers and honeyeaters flitted among the treetops, feeding.

Through the feathery branches I looked across a small gully to a knife-edged ridge that jutted out into the main valley, its steeply sloping sides blanketed with a green patchwork quilt of fallow sweet-potato plots. Dark mountains formed a foreboding backdrop where they walled in the Heluk River that roared unseen southwards through a narrow canyon in its tortuous journey to places beyond.

Suddenly I was aware of a figure running along the ridge in our direction. At this time of the morning—not yet six a.m.—the runner must have travelled through the night from some village in the south, and since he was in haste, he must bear urgent news. As I watched the person near, I recognized his gait. It was Arelek, who had become a friend of mine. I knew he had been visiting friends at Holuwon. I slipped on a pair of shoes and went outside to meet him.

Panting, he blurted out, "The people of Nendanggin and Fuplim have made new ancestral fetishes and they have killed Olondeng, the Christian chief! They say they are opposed to God's words and will kill anyone who comes near their village, whether one of the Danis, you or Bruno. Yesterday Olondeng set out to warn you, so they ambushed him on the mountain trail and we hear that they killed him. Now, my older brother, I have come here today to warn you."

By this time, a crowd of men had gathered around us and on hearing this, they began to shout the news to the surrounding hamlets and villages. Their whooping yodel carried well in the confines of our rocky valley and the clear mountain air, so in no time at all the message had been spread to the furthest villages of the Ninia area. I still find it hard to believe that within half an hour, groups of men, all fully armed with bows and arrows, had arrived from villages which took me a full hour to reach. "We have gathered in response to this news, and we are ready to go to Holuwon to protect our brothers and sisters there," they said.

Yali Warriors

In the meantime, when Bruno heard the uproar, he called some of us into his house to discuss and pray over the news. That was typical Bruno. On his desk was a small wooden plaque with the words "pray first" engraved on it. We prayed together, then Bruno reminded us, "We are under the authority of the Indonesian government." Above the murmuring of some of the Yalis who were restless to get going, he added, "And we are obliged to inform the police at Wamena of the alleged killing."

While everyone waited impatiently, Bruno called the MAF pilot based in the highland town of Wamena on the shortwave radio. He explained what we knew and asked the pilot to relay the information to the police office. Eventually, it was determined that the police wanted to fly to Ninia to meet with Bruno and me first, and then proceed to Holuwon and conduct an investigative patrol. However, the waiting Yali men—some Christians, but many not—decided not to delay a minute longer, but set off on their own to provide protection for believers and relatives there. "These people have made ancestral fetishes and that can only mean one thing," they explained. "There are going to be killings!"

That day, as we waited for the police officers to arrive, Yariut, who helped in our house, came to me with evident concern. "You need to wear a war vest." He used the Yali word *sing,* the specific term for a piece of traditional armour made by the Yali men from tightly woven rattan—a stone-age version of the modern Kevlar bulletproof vest—and strong enough to protect one's vital organs from the average war arrow.

"I don't have one," I replied, thinking that was the end of the matter.

"In that case, John," he said with all seriousness, "You must put on two or three sweaters so that when the arrows hit you, they will not go in too deep!" That is how I came to be sitting on the bank of the Heluk River that fateful day, with Indonesian policemen firing their rifles in the air, fearful that I or others could get killed and anxious about my young family at Ninia.[13]

Despite the evident hostility on the opposite side of the river, by midafternoon, the bridge had been completed, pole by pole, and

---

13 See opening chapter, A Decisive Day.

secured with vines. One by one we gingerly crossed and began to wend our way up the canyon wall through the stunted trees and undergrowth. No one expected an attack here. However, as dusk was falling, we had to pass through an open savannah just below the village where we were headed. This was the place where it was presumed we would be ambushed, but we passed through unchallenged and began the final ascent up the limestone hill to Nendanggin.

The huts stood silent and empty, but shouts drew our attention to a knot of armed men standing on the ridge above the village. "Don't shoot us," they called from their vantage point. "We remember what the police did in the Seng Valley when Stan Dale was killed by the people there; don't do that to us!"

They alluded to a tragedy following the murders of the missionaries in 1968. Some Indonesian police had hiked over the mountain from Ninia into the Seng River Valley, intending to capture the culprits and bring them to justice. They had arrested and shut up several suspects in a Yali hut, but when the captured men panicked and attempted to break out by tearing apart the wall boards, a couple of belligerent or trigger-happy policemen had opened fire with automatic weapons and riddled the wooden hut with bullets.

With Bruno acting as interpreter, the police assured the Nendanggin men that they were safe. "We have only come to speak with you. Let us spend the night in your village, and tomorrow we will talk." Some of the Yali men who were with us approached them unarmed and urged them to come and meet with us. In the ensuing conversation, we learned that Olondeng had not been killed but beaten, and though left for dead, would apparently recover.

That night, sleep was fitful. Bruno, I and a number of Yali men were packed so tightly in the village's large round "sacred" hut that we couldn't stretch out our legs, never mind lie down. But even if we had been able, our thoughts were overwhelmed with emotions and memories of the events of the day, and whenever we dozed off we were soon disturbed by unwanted dreams or cramping in our legs.

The next morning, we sat in the open space between the huts while the Indonesian police officers investigated the beating of the Christian chief and addressed the issue of the murderous threats the Nendanggin people had made against the Dani evangelists, Yali believers and us missionaries. Finally, with Bruno interpreting from Indonesian to Yali, the patrol leader told them, "You are under the authority and protection of the government of Indonesia. Because the government has given permission for these missionaries to come here, you must not hinder or threaten them in any way, and when they come here, you must welcome them and provide hospitality."

As we returned with lighter hearts to Ninia, I silently pondered what exactly God had meant when he spoke to me on the bank of the Heluk River:"You will live and do the work I brought you here to do, and you will not leave until it is finished."

CHAPTER 9

New Frontiers

I followed the muddy bare feet of the Yali in front of me as our party plodded, head-down and increasingly weary, through the enervating heat and humidity of the lowland forest. I should have been paying more attention to my surroundings. Here there were no spectacular vistas such as I might enjoy on a mountain track, but our trail wound between magnificent tropical giants with buttress roots as wide as a garage door, others with their trunks bound by strangler figs, and some draped with the kinds of liana that dangle tantalizingly—the kind Tarzan would swing from. Narrow, steamy beams of midday sunlight slanted through the forest canopy a hundred feet or more above our heads, while at our feet, ants and lizards scavenged in the decomposing layer of vegetation and humus on the forest floor.

All this was just a blur in my peripheral vision as I trudged along, almost lulled to sleep by the heat and the mind-numbing monotony. Suddenly, there was a great burst of excited whooping up ahead and the sound of people crashing through undergrowth towards a sunlit clearing where a slow-moving stream flowed.

I was too slow to see all the action. The early bird catches the worm, and it was the alert man at the head of the line who saw the huge green python sunbathing on a low branch overhanging the creek. The Dani evangelist Pubu, in a lightning-fast reaction, had fired successive arrows with amazing accuracy into its head and torso. Then he and some companions dived into the water to wrestle with the still powerfully writhing snake and bring it onto dry land. Once sure it was dead, they coiled it up like a thick green fire hose and tied it with vine so that one man could sling it over his shoulder and carry it with us for the evening meal.

This was to be our third night since leaving Ninia, and at our bivouac at who knows where in the lowland jungle that night, snake steak supplemented our simple rations.

☙

Shortly after the incident at Nendanggin, Bruno and his wife Marlys had reluctantly decided that they and their young family must return to Canada. Their only daughter, who had had meningitis as an infant, was now suffering seizures and also showing signs of learning disability.

We would miss their company and comradeship in our isolated mountain outpost. We'd miss Bruno's wit, wisdom and winsome spirit, and with the work increasing in nature and scope, we were faced with a challenge. The incipient Yali church was starting to grow, and it was crucial that its young members be taught and its illiterate elders trained. Moreover, the emerging church was already a boldly witnessing church, so the boundaries of the work were expanding into the valleys east and west, and southwards beyond the lower reaches of the Heluk River Valley. A solitary missionary couple for this vast area and the far-flung Yali population was not going to be enough. How could we meet this challenge?

In the few months remaining to him, however, Bruno was bent on fulfilling some of his dreams. One was to establish a foothold for the gospel in the lowlands among an isolated tribal group whom the Yali people had traditionally called "Somahai."[14] The initiative to seek out the lowlanders partly came from Bruno's dear friends, the Dani evangelists, but it was also due to the efforts of a man called Belak.

Belak was the chief of Uwam, the most southerly and lowest-lying cluster of Yali hamlets. A stocky, powerfully built man, he was disarmingly gentle and soft-spoken, with a slightly husky voice. "I was a small boy, perhaps five or six years old," he told me, "when a plane landed on the Balim River in the lowlands below Uwam. It brought a party of white men, who hiked up into the mountains where they made their base camp beside our village. One day, while the village elders watched with apprehension, the strange, pale visitors dressed me in clothes and fed me some of

14 The correct name for these people is Momina, but at that time we only knew what the Yali called them.

their peculiar food. Some thought, 'Maybe they want to adopt Belak and take him away.' Others said, 'Perhaps they will kill him with poison.' But they treated me well, and I was unafraid, just curious."

"When I was still young," he continued, "I used to hear legends about an ancestor called Ké-ani who had wandered in the lowlands on a hunting trip. On one occasion, when he was about to cross a small river, he realized that a band of armed Somahai men were standing rock-still on the other bank, silently watching him. Naturally, Ké-ani was very nervous, but improvising sign language, he gesticulated that he was alone except for his hunting dog and offered gifts of fresh-killed meat from his net bag to break the tension. When the tall lowlanders invited him to cross the river, he waded cautiously to the other side and shared his food with them. In subsequent visits, Ké-ani traded and hunted with the Somahai people and even learned to speak some of their words."

After a reflective pause, Belak went on. "I always wanted to renew contact with the Somahai, but something happened before I could do that. When I was a teenager, an old man in the village prophesied, 'Some day, foreigners will come into our valley speaking a strange language and bringing words which will differ from those passed down by our ancestors. When they come, you will give up the old ways and the traditions passed down to us by the ancestors. You will learn this new tradition which the strangers will bring.'

"No one knew what that meant, but years later when I was already a young man, we heard that white strangers had come to Ninia who did not speak our language, and then I heard rumours that a man from the Dani tribe called Pubu had come. Though he was dark-skinned like us, he did not speak our language, but had come to live in the village of Yalisili. They said he was telling the people a strange new message.

"When I heard this, I remembered the prophecy I had heard as a boy, and resolved to make the journey through the forest, avoiding our enemies at Nendanggin, in order to visit Yalisili and find out about this teaching. As Pubu spoke and a Yali from Ninia interpreted his words into our language, I became convinced this was what had been foretold in the prophecy. One night I urged him, 'Please come to my village,' and when he agreed, I insisted he make a clear promise. 'After how many sleeps will you come? I need to know so that I can tell my people to prepare for your visit.'"

☙

The day came when the Dani evangelist, Pubu, arrived with his Yali interpreter at Uwam to a warm reception by an excited crowd. He was astonished to see that bundles of bows and arrows and various kinds of sacred objects, charms and fetishes, had been gathered and piled up with wood ready for burning. It reminded Pubu of what had happened some years earlier back in his home village near Karubaga far to the west.

"When I saw that pile ready for burning," Pubu had told me, when I researched the story, "I remembered how the missionaries had restrained us from burning our fetishes until we heard and understood the *obeelom wone*—the good news. So, just like those missionaries, I pleaded with Belak to wait, but I could hardly restrain him because he and the people were determined at that instant to give up their old traditions and learn the new words and the new ways. All I could do was persuade them to wait a few days so I could begin to teach them the gospel of new life in Jesus Christ."

Before the week was out, the Uwam people under Belak's leadership could not be restrained any longer. They lit the huge bonfire that had been prepared in advance, burned up their sacred objects and amulets, and closed a chapter on their former belief system and way of life driven by fear of spirits, constant enmity, and the imperative to reciprocate and exact revenge.

Belak was resolved that the gospel must be passed on to the lowland people. He began to venture further and further into the lowland forest until at last he re-established friendly contact with the people he knew as Somahai. Because of Belak, we were now on this exploratory trek into the uncharted lowlands of Papua.

☙

After a supper of roasted python and boiled rice in our jungle camp on the edge of Somahai territory, tired out from our third twelve-hour day of hiking, Bruno and I were glad to crawl into our makeshift shelter. But I didn't sleep well that night. It wasn't just our aching limbs and the lack of a comfortable bed or the tropical storm which crashed in the forest around us, it was also the excitement that in the morning we might come face to face with some Somahai people.

How would that meeting be? In the restlessness of that night I half-dreamed, half-hoped there would be a welcome. But what if the reception was less than welcoming or even hostile? Surely not, since Belak would be our go-between.

Everyone was up with the first filtered rays of sunlight slanting on us through the tree canopy, eager to set off on the final leg of our journey. Belak, and others who knew the way, led us southeast. We waded along a shallow meandering stream for half an hour and then cut off into the forest again. About three hours later we emerged beside a wide river—actually two rivers where they came together—which after the rainstorm of the night was very full. As we waded across, the water became deeper and deeper until it was chest high, and our shorter Dani and Yali companions were forced to carry their loads on their heads.

Pubu came alongside me. He was one of the shortest men with us and the water was already up to his chin. He just grinned at me, and raising his pack high over his head, took a big breath and kept walking until only his arms were visible, moving like a periscope through the water. Then his head reappeared—he had passed the deepest point—still grinning.

As we dried out and reorganized ourselves on the other bank, two men suddenly appeared before us. They were trembling, their eyes bulging from excitement and obvious apprehension, while beads of perspiration ran down their faces. They stood taller than the mountain men and were naked except for a strategically placed leaf. Tufts of their dirty hair were tied with white orchid fibre, a small piece of bamboo passed horizontally through their nasal septa, and bat-wing bones sprouted from each side of their noses like a cat's whiskers. We were the first white men they had seen, and no doubt we seemed as bizarre to them as they did to us.

The two Somahai men who suddenly appeared

We were apprehensive too, uncertain of our welcome. However, after they talked with Belak, they led us directly to a clearing where we found a community of twenty-seven men, women and children living together in a single, rustic longhouse, constructed on top of the trunk of a large fallen tree. As a token of hospitality, they immediately offered us food—plantains baked in the ashes of the fire, slightly charred and covered with ash. I was about to peel mine when I noticed that one of the local men smacked his with a cupped hand to knock off some of the ash, but then popped the entire thing into his mouth unpeeled. Bruno and I looked at each other and, with the terse comment, "When in Rome..." followed their example. The ice was broken, and there were smiles all round.

The trip was exploratory. Bruno wanted to know if we could establish a new frontier for the gospel among the Somahai people. He hoped to ascertain if they would welcome someone to come and live among them, and if there was a suitable piece of land to build an airstrip, which could serve as a base for evangelism.

My goal was to find out if the language of these lowland folk was related in any way to Yali or one of the other mountain languages. Over the next few days, camped in that clearing, I was able to compile an extensive word list. I discovered that the speech of these lowlanders was tonal and quite unrelated to the Yali language. We also paced out a piece of land nearby and determined that there was a length suitable for an airstrip, provided we lined it up with the river which would allow a clear approach or takeoff.

Our party's food supplies were running low and we still faced four days of hiking to get back up to Ninia. As we tramped home, Bruno and I were overjoyed and excited at the possibility of expanding the scope of the work—but I could not help wondering what it would take to bring the gospel to these lowlanders and in particular, what I would be able to do without Bruno's support and help.

CHAPTER 10

A Few Good Men

"John, if you do nothing else here among the Yali but invest in a few faithful men like these, you will have an effective ministry."

Bruno de Leeuw and his family were gone, and Gloria and I were enjoying a short visit by Ernest W. Oliver, the UK director of our mission. He made this observation as we walked back to the house after the Friday-morning meeting with a group of Yali elders.

Newly literate and even illiterate men were emerging as the first leaders of the fledgling Yali church. Our practice was to appoint men to leadership quickly—often, in those days, as soon as they were baptized, provided they demonstrated the right qualities of character and potential—so Bruno initiated this custom of a Friday-morning meeting to help train and equip them. We would meet in the open, on a small grassy knoll beside the airstrip, for fellowship, prayer and teaching.

Most of these church leaders walked the short distance from their villages around Ninia—perhaps an hour or maybe an hour and a half away—and it was no hardship for them. However, a few of them came to the meeting from further afield. For example, each Thursday, two unpretentious and somewhat reticent men, Elabo Munap and Elabo Holohobim, left their homes in Holuwon at the south end of the valley and hiked for six or seven hours to Ninia. They participated in the Friday worship and teaching, then, in the afternoon, started the long hike home to share what they had learned with their people.

That is easy to say, but this is a land where journeys are measured by travel time rather than as the crow flies. I knew that trail well, and the first time I made the hike, it took me all of twelve hours—one way.

On another occasion, along with a few Yali companions, I set out from Holuwon to head up valley to Ninia. It was before dawn, when the air was cool, and the dew on the grasses soaked my legs and trickled down into my socks. Moisture-bejewelled cobwebs festooned the trail, but with my head down to see where to place my feet, I rarely noticed them until I felt their dew and tacky gossamer across my face. I found myself wishing the Yali men were taller than me—then I'd get them to break trail!

Immediately we began the first five-hundred-meter climb up into the dripping rainforest. As first light filtered through the trees, I heard the crystal-clear pings of unseen frogs in the damp mosses beside the trail and the musical piping of wrens and flower-peckers foraging in the wet branches overhead. The path contoured round the mountain before it descended into the next side valley and out into open garden land. Too soon for me we were climbing again at the forest's edge and between garden plots, then steeply up a cliff, following narrow ledges of loose shale, where the drop was thankfully obscured by bushes, mountain rhododendron and stands of a reed-like bamboo. By that time, the sun was over the ranges and beginning to banish the morning mists in the treetops, and my escorts were anxious to be over the next crest, pass through two large villages, and re-enter the rainforest before the sun's noonday intensity began to beat down on our necks.

Once over the highest point in our journey, we were soon winding our way back down, crisscrossing streams and passing through a fertile garden area that sloped down towards the Heluk River. My friends showed me where the two Yali believers Yeikwaroho and Bingguok were martyred and where Stan Dale was shot in 1966. We crossed the surging waters of the Heluk on a swaying vine suspension bridge and made good time through the bush near the water's edge, but then a cliff forced us to cross back over the fast-paced river on a precarious, cantilevered pole bridge. The rough pathway now climbed steadily as the Heluk River roared past us, and at times I had to scramble over slippery rocks or even wade through the river's shallows. I visualized how painfully gruelling this must have been for Stan Dale with five arrows in his body. Endlessly up and down, the tortuous path led on through a dank gorge where waterfalls cascaded hundreds of feet on either side, their constant spray glistening in the sunlight and soaking the moss-covered rocks and trees.

Finally, we came to the base of a ridge. I didn't know where to find the energy necessary for the last three-hundred-meter climb up a white zigzagging path in the limestone that disappeared into the gathering afternoon mists above us. But I summoned up my last reserves and, fortified with the knowledge that I would soon be home, I plodded step by weary step upwards to Ninia.

The two Elabos used to make this journey in *both* directions every week. In time, through their unassuming faithfulness, they helped establish the church in Holuwon.

☙

EWO, as we affectionately knew the British director, had been a missionary in India, but by this time was widely regarded in England as a "missionary statesman." We were privileged to have a visit from this godly, wise and knowledgeable man and his wife. I recognized that his advice echoed the apostle Paul's counsel to Timothy: "The things you have heard me say in the presence of many witnesses entrust to reliable men who will also be qualified to teach others."[15]

These words were to become the lodestar of my life and work in Papua. They were reinforced when I read *Missionary Methods: Saint Paul's or Ours?*—a classic written half a century earlier by Roland Allen, who bemoaned the failure of his contemporaries to

---

15 Author's paraphrase of 2 Timothy 2:2.

train and release local Christians into ministry. This, he claimed, demonstrated a double lack of trust: a failure to trust the Holy Spirit to influence and lead the emerging leaders, and an almost arrogant lack of trust in their innate ability and potential.

Allen wrote, "We have educated our converts to put us in the place of Christ. We believe that it is the Holy Spirit of Christ which inspires and guides us: we cannot believe that the same Spirit will guide and inspire them. We believe that the Holy Spirit has taught us and is teaching us true conceptions of morality, doctrine, ritual: we cannot believe that the same Spirit will teach them."[16]

Later I heard a slightly different perspective from an American missionary colleague. In a brief paper circulated to colleagues in his mission agency, he contended, "Most missionaries expect to phase themselves *out* of the work at some point, at least before they leave; however, they ought to be proactively phasing nationals *into* leadership from the beginning."[17]

With the combined wisdom of these veteran missionaries, I realized I needed a plan not only to phase myself out, but also a strategy to mobilize local people into ministry leadership from the very start. Although a missionary is well aware of the temporary nature of his or her own role, by adopting a "phase-out" posture,

16 Roland Allen, *Missionary Methods: St. Paul's or Ours?,* Eerdmans, Michigan, 1962:143-144.

17 John Ellenberger, missionary with the Christian and Missionary Alliance. Author's recollection.

he or she doesn't go far enough. The danger is one ends up in a pastoral role, doing what the national can and should be trained to do.

The missionary role is essentially apostolic and transitional, not settled and pastoral. It is therefore foundational and facilitative. I learned to respect my local brothers or sisters as equals in any ministry task. I honoured their inherent ability and sought to develop their potential to lead the fledgling church with the enabling of the Holy Spirit. Mr. Oliver was absolutely right.

☙

Long before Bruno left for Canada it was intended that Gloria and I would settle in Holuwon to oversee the ministry in the thirteen southern Yali villages. The population was not much larger than that around Ninia, but the distances between the villages were much greater and the terrain more rugged. Besides, people coming from the southeast were forced to cross the Heluk River at a point where no permanent bridge could be built. Most of the time, the only link was a flimsy pole bridge constructed from boulder to boulder. In flash floods, though, this could be suddenly swept away and accidents could happen. On one occasion, a young man was swept to his death while others looked on, powerless to help, as the surging current hurled his body against the rocks.

There were other ways of bridging this otherwise impassable river. One was to build a vine suspension bridge, and another to use a *hohwa,* a kind of jungle breeches buoy. This consisted of a hoop of rattan around a vine strung high above the river. The intrepid traveller would wedge his feet and knees into the hoop and, leaning backward, pull himself across the chasm hand over hand.

However, both the suspension bridge and the *hohwa* required anchor points high enough on each of the banks where there would be no fear of erosion; but in the relentless heat and humidity the vines would rot and become unsafe within a year. As I thought about these factors, it seemed obvious that it was unrealistic to expect elders to come to Holuwon for training every week from the far-flung villages—especially those east of the river. The distances were too great and the dangers too real.

Instead of a weekly meeting, after discussion with the church leaders, I initiated a monthly seminar. The elders soon accepted the habit of gathering the afternoon before the seminar began. We hosted them in several huts around the village, so the leaders came, just as they were, without any need to bring food or firewood. In the evening, they joined in the nightly hut meetings around the fire and shared in or led the worship—singing Yali hymns, reciting from memory a verse of Scripture, or offering a devotional talk and prayer. Early the following morning we met together for an entire day filled with worship, prayer, Bible teaching and study. One important feature of the seminar was an open session where we discussed the specific pastoral issues they confronted in the villages and they learned to find answers in the Scriptures.

Although the ability to read was not initially a requirement for church leadership, most of the men who were chosen to serve were newly literate or at least enrolled in literacy training. However, that didn't mean they could read fluently in such a way that people could enjoy listening to the reading! Of course, the Yali belong to an oral culture, used to learning by listening; but it was one thing to listen to a well-told Yali story and another altogether to try to make sense of someone's stuttering and stumbling reading of a foreign text—which the Bible was.

How Gloria and I taught the people to read and write, and how the Bible was eventually translated so it could be read aloud to these natural listeners is a story in itself. Meanwhile, in the monthly elders' seminars I introduced reading drills to develop confidence and fluency in reading aloud for the enjoyment and benefit of the hearers.

In this way, month by month over the next fifteen years, the elders (and some of their wives with them) grew in their knowledge of the Word of God and their ability to lead the believers in their care. So when eventually the day came for us to leave, we did so, confident that more than a few faithful men and women would carry on the work of the ministry.

CHAPTER 11

Holuwon

I am getting ahead of myself. I need to help you connect a few more dots, and to do that I have to go back to when we arrived in Papua in 1971 and settled initially among the Dani people in Karubaga, before moving to Ninia in 1972.

Gloria and I had assumed that upon arrival we would be assigned by the leadership to a specific location and to language study. However, we soon discovered otherwise during our orientation by the Dutch-Canadian field leader, John Dekker. "We want to be sensitive to how God might lead in your lives, and though you are initially to be based here at Karubaga and will start to learn the Dani language, I encourage you to consider a number of options before the field conference in April."

Korupun was a case in point. In December, a Mission Aviation Fellowship plane was scheduled to take us to this most remote and inaccessible of the villages where RBMU was working at that time. Our forty-five-minute flight from Karubaga first climbed high over the mountains before entering the hidden "Shangri-La" valley where the Balim River meanders across a former lakebed completely encircled by a wall of limestone mountains.

This secluded valley was discovered by the modern world during World War II when American airmen carried out a risky rescue of the survivors of a plane crash. Now our mission plane, flown by an American pilot, traversed the extensive and fertile plain with its savannah, patchwork quilts of humped sweet-potato gardens and scattered hamlets of low, grass-roofed huts. At the eastern end of the broad valley, over unnumbered centuries, the river has carved its way through the mountains and now thrusts and tumbles its way rapidly downwards through a winding fifty-kilometer gorge until it spills out onto the southern lowlands.

Our single-engined plane now veered east, away from the Balim Valley, following a course close to the steep rocky spurs of the central cordillera until it finally headed north into a narrow valley. Just when we thought there was nowhere to go, with mountains looming ahead, the pilot abruptly banked steeply to the right again—the wingtip seeming too close to precipitous crags and moss-draped treetops—then just as unexpectedly swung left into a box canyon. There, tucked between walls of rock and streaming waterfalls, we saw a small patch of green with clusters of round huts from which smoke spiralled upwards. Before we knew it, the plane was safely down, bumping and rattling up the uneven grass strip at Korupun.

Americans Paul and Kathryn Kline welcomed us into their simple home among the pygmy-sized Kimyal people. The first resident missionary among them had been murdered along with Stan Dale in the Seng Valley a few years previously, and now the Klines had been making inroads into the language. The Korupun folk are short and wiry but what they lack in size is compensated by their aggressive, irascible personalities. Only a few months earlier several people had been shot with arrows in an ongoing feud and some had died, so the tensions were still there. The Kimyal were not easy to work with and their environment was not only remote but inhospitable and oppressive. Paul and Kathryn had been longing for someone to join them there for companionship and to share the burden of this tough assignment.

One day, while we were listening with them to the crackling shortwave radio—the missionaries' lifeline for news and flight information—we heard the guttural Dutch accent of Bruno de Leeuw. "A crew of Dani volunteers has just completed the airstrip at Holuwon. Could you come over, Paul? I need help to fix the shovels and wheelbarrows before sending them over the trail to another airstrip site in the next valley."

Paul was a jack of all trades and master of many. He was a truly all-round missionary who built houses, repaired gasoline engines, and fixed all things mechanical from watches to wheelbarrows. "Gloria and John are here as our guests," mild-mannered Paul explained. "I don't feel it right to walk out on them, Bruno."

"Bring John with you," Bruno urged gently. "I can really use the help, and it will be just for one night. I'll pay the costs of the flights."

So, leaving our wives together at Korupun, Paul and I were flown by MAF plane the twenty minutes to Holuwon, where we landed smoothly on the newly opened, steep yellow clay strip. It was a hot, humid day. The sun beat down from a cloudless, azure sky, and by the time we gathered for the night in a little wooden shack, we were sunburned, tired and thirsty.

I was delighted to meet Bruno, who was based up-valley at Ninia and whose name I already knew from Stan Dale's writings, which I had seen before leaving Britain. That evening I reflected on what he had told me about the area and the work among the Yali. "Holuwon has been identified as a potential site for a Bible school," Bruno had explained, "and some funds are already available. However, at present, as you see, it is a deserted spot—the only huts are the temporary homes of the men who constructed the airstrip. The nearest Yali village is about a thirty-minute walk up the valley and another, Yalisili, about an hour's climb up the mountain. Nevertheless, a few days ago I baptized eleven young Christians—the first in the area."

During the day I had taken time to look around and take stock of the situation. Holuwon was a sloping plateau—a vast slab of sandstone like a tilted, shallow saucer—that some unseen volcanic force had hoisted up between the Heluk and Balim Rivers. The top edge abutted a mountain but most of its southern and eastern rim consisted of sheer sandstone cliffs that dropped down towards the two rivers. Its entire surface was covered by a layer of heavy yellowish clay laced with white sand. The land seemed surprisingly infertile; the vegetation which normally would be lush and prolific in this tropical climate was stunted and scraggly, but not without beauty and colour. I saw pink and golden orchids, red bromeliads, and yellow rhododendron. Waxy red leaves of one kind of tree were translucently vivid in the sunlight. Occasionally butterflies flitted by—large white ones, their wings marked with orange "eyes," and swallowtails of iridescent blue.

The view from Holuwon was spectacular. Forested ridges and huge rocky crags were visible from northwest to southeast. Far off to the south, visible through the V-shaped Balim Valley, sea-blue lowlands stretched to the horizon about eighty kilometers away.

Nevertheless, when I returned to Korupun, I gave Gloria my overwhelming impression: "It is a desolate place—no one lives there, according to Bruno, because the local Yali people believe it is the domain of malicious spirits. The land is basically a desert, with scrubby vegetation and white sand everywhere reflecting the hot sun. You could never plant a garden and grow vegetables or fruit there. There are no villages nearby, and as I looked out over the forest, there were none visible to the naked eye." In short, Holuwon did not appeal to me.

Nonetheless, in some mysterious way, God laid this apparently uninviting place on our hearts, and when we met with the field leadership at our first field conference, we told them we had prayed over the ensuing weeks and had each concluded that God wanted us there. The leadership committee decided to allocate us to Holuwon, but thoughtfully recommended we first go to Ninia to learn the Yali language and to be mentored by Bruno. When they brought this recommendation to the field members for open discussion the vote was unanimous, and welcomed with an excited round of applause. "We have never had such unanimity over any previous allocation," someone explained.

With this vote of confidence, we had moved to Ninia, made a good beginning in the Yali language, and then, following our first home leave in Britain, were ready to move down the valley from Ninia to make our home in Holuwon. By nature I am a team player, though, so before we made the move, I called together three of my Yali friends—emerging leaders I had come to love and trust—and asked them, "Would one of you be willing to leave your extended family here and join me in opening the work at Holuwon?"

Erariek, Luliap and Enggiahap (1972)

They looked surreptitiously at each other, waiting to see who would speak first. Each of them knew at least three tribal languages, had studied at the Dani Bible school in Karubaga, and had expressed interest in translating the Bible.

Luliap was the one I knew best. He was not only a highly intelligent man, but wise and good-natured, with an abundant sense of humour. He had been a close companion of Stan Dale and had caught from him a vision for translating the Scriptures into Yali. I knew we would get on well together, and in my heart of hearts I hoped he would volunteer.

Erariek was a very bright and quick-witted man, brimming with enthusiasm, creativity and initiative—always thinking "outside the box" and skilled with his hands. He would be useful to have around at the start of the work when there were practical things to do, and he would be sure to help find a solution to problems. I felt he too could be a great companion and colleague. He also bubbled with humour and always seemed to have a twinkle in his eye.

The third man was Enggiahap—his name means "fingernail". On first impression he was a little shy, even morose, and perhaps overshadowed by the other two. However, when I first arrived at Ninia, he had hiked around the valley with me, showing me the different trails and shortcuts, pointing out springs with tasty fresh water, and teaching me new vocabulary. I sensed he was a quiet, thoughtful and reliable person who would stick with me through thick and thin. But up to this point, I had not seen the great potential behind his withdrawn demeanour.

After some hesitation Luliap explained that he felt he should remain at Ninia. I think he felt that, with Bruno now gone, he needed to be there. He also saw that the pioneering role of the Dani evangelists was coming to an end, which meant that people like him had to be ready to step in and assume greater responsibility and leadership. Erariek also had an acceptable excuse. He had already told me he hoped to go on to further education. Enggiahap had remained silent up to this point, but finally he lifted his head and said quietly but with unmistakeable resolve, "I will go!"

There were many practical things to do at Holuwon in those pioneering days, and Enggiahap proved to be a willing and hard worker—ready for anything from building or making a path to creatively fixing a broken chair. He even proved to be a capable assistant to Gloria in a medical crisis, able to suture wounds with a regular needle and thread and to give penicillin injections.

We worked well together, sharing responsibilities and helping each other when pastoral issues inevitably arose. I combined my knowledge of the Scriptures with his insights and understanding of the culture's intricacies, but even then we needed wisdom from God to know how to handle them, so we prayed together.

Enggiahap also began to show his leadership potential, influencing and guiding people as much by example as by charisma, which he certainly had, but also with his consultative style and his timely and wise words. Inevitably, this was recognized by others and eventually he was recalled to Ninia to serve as head of the growing church district there. Even so, by the time Enggiahap left Holuwon, we had an incipient church with a cadre of inexperienced but teachable elders who were beginning to take on more responsibility for spiritual oversight. Our task was to keep on training these men at Holuwon and the twelve scattered villages around us.

I found that my heart was divided. Although we had only spent about three years at Ninia, it was there we had learned the language and made our first, lasting Yali friends. But when we moved to Holuwon, we were making a fresh start—like young people who must leave home and begin to work as adults, finding their way in the world and establishing new relationships.

After some years I said to my Yali friends, *"O Ninia etma re an endag-napswa famen de, o Holuwon suma re an log atihik"* (Though I was raised at Ninia, it was here in Holuwon I grew to adulthood). It was in Holuwon that Gloria and I were to bring up our family, and have some of the most satisfying, productive—and, to be honest, sometimes frustrating—years of ministry.

The view from Holuwon

CHAPTER 12

The Gospel at Work

Wesen was furious. "I am going to divorce my wife!" he declared.

This news took me completely by surprise. Wesen was an intelligent young man with a ready smile, down-to-earth manner, and a quick-witted mind. Though he was not the brightest flame in the growing community of Christians at Holuwon, he was faithful and eager to grow in his understanding of what it meant to be a disciple of Jesus.

His wife Wasel was a pretty young woman with a pleasant demeanour. I had never heard of any trouble or strife in their four or five years of marriage, which was unusual in the average Yali household, so I was puzzled. I enquired of some friends what had brought about this dramatic turn of events that had become the buzz of the community. I discovered it was a very unusual incident.

Wesen, who occasionally worked for me as a carpenter, was one of the few people in the village who had enough money to purchase an aluminium cooking pot in which Wasel usually cooked sweet-potato leaves for him each evening. One afternoon when she was about to prepare the evening meal, her little boy Sabu began to urinate on the hut floor, so without thinking, she grabbed the cooking pot and held it in front of him. It happened that some other women had seen the incident through the open doorway, so when Wesen returned from working in his garden they told him, "We saw your wife allow your son Sabu to pee into your cooking pot, and then she cooked your vegetables in the same pot!"

He was outraged, as any typical Yali might be. Although the Yali people had little idea about hygiene and of course knew nothing about germs, they were very particular about avoiding contact with bodily excreta, so the thought of his wife then cooking his potato leaves in that same pot was unthinkable. To compound matters, his family, who were not Christians, soon heard about the incident and joined the fray. "Rid yourself of that good-for-nothing woman," they told him angrily. "She has brought shame on you and on us. Get rid of her, and we will find you a wife who is worthy of you!"

Enggiahap and I tried talking to Wesen, but not only was the whole affair personally odious and offensive to him, he was also feeling enormous social pressure from his family. After all, they had helped him with the bride price, as was the custom, probably contributing several large live pigs. Clearly they had a stake in his marriage, so whatever they had to say carried weight with the offended man. It appeared to me that he was not to be dissuaded from divorcing the mother of his two small children.

However, I had an idea. I believed that through prayer and with guidance from God's Word, we might be able to help Wesen grow spiritually through this testing experience. Since he was literate, I suggested he read Ephesians 5, which Enggiahap and I had recently translated. I showed him the passage. "Wesen, my younger brother, I would like you to read this passage and then pray and think about it for a few days. Then come back and talk to me about what you think those verses mean."

A couple of days later, Wesen casually showed up at my ever-open office door and I invited him inside. He had his draft copy of Ephesians in his hand, so I asked him, "Did you read the verses I showed you, my younger brother? And did you understand them?"

"Yes, older brother, I read them. I read those words where Paul said that Jesus loves his people the church even though we have our defects and sins, but he desires to present us to God in perfect condition."

"That's good, my friend, you have truly understood what Paul said. How do you think this applies to you, since your wife offended you?"

"I read that we husbands must love our wives the same way Jesus loves us, and that means I must love my wife even with her faults and all the wrong things she does. It is clear, older brother, that I must still love my wife even though she did this offensive thing to me. I cannot listen to my family's advice; I must do what God tells me in his Word."

And Wesen did just that.

ଓ

The abduction of a teenage girl by a headstrong youth, marital troubles and wife beating were common pastoral issues Enggiahap and I had to deal with. One day, when the elders from all over the area had gathered for our monthly seminar and we were about to begin, we heard a woman's piercing screams from somewhere in the middle of the village. "What's that screaming all about?" I asked.

"Oh, that's just Atiut beating his wife," someone explained casually.

"Go ahead with your prayer and worship," I instructed, as I headed to the classroom door. "I'm going to find out what's going on."

Atiut was one of our elders and should have been in the seminar, but obviously he had more pressing family matters to attend to! I had known him for a few years. He was a likeable young man with a ready smile, a serious mind, an aptitude for teaching and a willingness to learn. We often joked together, but he had a red-hot temper—fiery and impetuous. His young wife Maratina was probably still a teenager, and though very personable, was quite immature and sometimes churlish. The two were a flammable mix.

I squeezed through the small doorway into their hut and paused for a moment, allowing my eyes to get used to the darkness. Maratina sat against the boards of the hut wall with her arms up protectively and tear streaks on her dusky face.

"What exactly is going on, Atiut?" I asked.

"Maratina will not do as I tell her, and the Bible says wives should obey their husbands, so I have been beating her. I know you understand, John, my older brother, that Yali women do not obey their husbands unless you beat them."

Drawing on my memory, fresh from translating Ephesians, I contradicted Atiut. "No, my young brother, it doesn't have to be like that. Yes, wives are told to submit to their husbands, but husbands are told to love their wives. God also teaches us to be patient and gentle, so don't think your wife will respect and obey you because you beat her. The opposite is true. She will love and obey you when you treat her with love and gentleness."

People don't change in a day, but Atiut had a responsive heart and was open to correction, and in time Maratina grew to be a loving and faithful wife—without enduring more beatings, and despite Atiut's quick temper.

ᏣᏰ

Occasionally, we had to deal with men wanting to take a second wife, problems between multiple wives, and of course adultery. Wiyeluen was a very attractive mother with a youthful face and figure that belied the fact that she already had three children. Her husband Yariut, who had begun working for us as a teenager when we lived at Ninia, came to the house one morning with a long face and a loud voice, filled with pent-up emotion. "My wife Wiyeluen has run off with that "incest-monger" Leila," he vented, using the strongest possible Yali idioms.[18]

Leila was quite handsome and manly by Yali standards, a natural leader who had also displayed considerable prowess in battle. He already had two wives and I could not understand what attracted Wiyeluen to him since she already had in Yariut a good, strong, hard-working husband, while Leila was a weasel of a man, renowned for his smooth-talking devious ways.

For a couple of days Yariut had pleaded in vain for her to return, but now he was asking for pastoral intervention. Enggiahap and I met first with Wiyeluen on her own and then with her husband, to see if she had any cause to be disgruntled with him, but it didn't seem so. Apparently it was nothing but an unreasonable infatuation with the other man, and nothing we said would persuade her that what she was doing was wrong. She was not

[18] Yariut used a term which is hard to translate. It's technical use is for a person who commits incest, but the term has deep religious connotations inferring incest brings a curse on everyone and everything. Yariut used it as the strongest derogatory term in Yali.

convicted of her sin. We tried to follow the procedure outlined in Matthew 18:15-17, attempting to get husband and wife to confess their faults to each other and be reconciled, but on Wiyeluen's part, there was not the slightest concession and not even a flicker of movement.

I had no previous experience with this kind of situation either in Britain or in Papua, but finally I made a suggestion. "Let us bring the case to the church, just as we read in Matthew 18. We will call a meeting of all the baptized members of the church and ask Wiyeluen to be present."

Yariut agreed to this, but several of the church members were astonished at my patently ill-conceived and unsound advice: "John, older brother, you have lived with us a long time and understand our culture. You know that will not work. Don't you know that her embarrassment and shame will keep her from coming before the entire church?"

Often I would bow to the wisdom of the Yalis, but not this time. "I do understand that, my brothers," I replied, "but this is the way God tells us to do it. If we do things God's way, we will know we are doing the right thing, even if Wiyeluen does not come to the meeting."

Everyone remained sceptical; nevertheless, on the appointed day we gathered in the literacy classroom which doubled as the church meeting place. We sang a few hymns, and after Elabo the pastor had prayed, I read the passage from Matthew and explained why we had gathered. Even then, a few people stated the obvious—"She hasn't come"—and a few pessimists added, "She won't come; she is too embarrassed."

Almost immediately, there was a knock on the door which had been wedged shut. Someone opened it and in walked Wiyeluen, her head hanging low in obvious shame. She stood humbly and dejectedly in front of the congregation. I asked, "My daughter, do you know why we are here and why we asked you to come?"

"Yes, my father. I have sinned against my husband and before God, and I have come to confess and reconcile with my husband. However, I ask, my father, that you send everyone here home and I will sit with you, the elders and my husband to determine what to do."

That day, Wiyeluen took the first steps of reconciliation with her husband, but it was more than that. From that point on she came alive as a Christian. She joined the literacy class, determined to read and learn what the Scriptures taught, and she went on to become one of the leading ladies in the women's fellowship group.

☙

Ten or so years after we had left Papua, I returned to give some Old Testament teaching to a group of Yali leaders. They arranged for me to stay in the old mission house Stan Dale had built at

Ninia which they had refurbished and made very comfortable, providing me with a mattress, sheets and blankets. I was on my own, but most nights my friends would come in and share a meal with me and sometimes I was invited to eat with them in their huts.

One Sunday morning I woke up feeling quite ill, with a bit of a fever, and when I got out of bed I felt dizzy and nauseous. I wasn't going anywhere, so I just flopped back on the bed. As I drifted in and out of sleep, I could hear the Yali hymn-singing in the church across the airstrip. Finally, I was conscious that church was over, and could hear the hum of voices and the laughter of children as the congregation stood outside in the warm sunshine chatting.

Soon I heard a gentle knock on the front door, followed by soft footsteps as someone cautiously approached the bedroom. It was Enggiahap. "My brother, I missed you at church this morning and figured you must be ill, so I came to find out," he explained, and then asked, "Have you eaten or drunk anything yet?"

When I told him I was too giddy and did not feel like eating, he went to the kitchen, made a pot of coffee, found some plain biscuits and brought them to me. While I sipped the hot, oversweet coffee, he sat on the end of the bed and started to talk. "It is not good to be on your own when you are sick, so I'll just sit here with you for a while. If you don't feel like talking, don't bother; but maybe after you get some of that coffee inside you, you'll feel better."

He started to reminisce about our early days together at Holuwon. During our first Christmas, there had been an outbreak of dysentery and his little boy Eminus had succumbed, passing away on Christmas Day. He recalled how I had gone over to his house and sat with him and his wife Esther, not saying much, just being present, showing I cared. He had appreciated that.

Then he began to recall incidents of our ministry together. "You know, older brother, we made a lot of mistakes in those days. We were both young and inexperienced, but God guided us and blessed the work, and now we can help the younger men and women who are coming into leadership."

I was touched that he had said "we" and not "you." It was an indication of true fellowship and confirmed my original strategy of working with and not over my national colleagues. I felt the same way he did; these men were every bit my equal and more.

CHAPTER 13

Raising Our Family in Papua

Gloria had gone to bed. It was January 1975, and we were still living in our little house at Ninia. I was up late talking with a group of men while we sat around the wood-burning stove. These were some of the Dani evangelists who were still working with us at that time. They had come from distant villages for a ministry refreshment conference and wanted to chat with me in the evening before leaving for the long hike home first thing in the morning.

Finally, about midnight—which is really late for people who normally go to sleep around nine o'clock—the last one left. I stoked fresh firewood in the firebox, closed the damper and filled two kettles, which I placed on the edge of the stove. It would ensure hot water for the morning cup of tea.

It seemed that I had barely fallen asleep when, in the pitch-black of the night, Gloria roused me. She was about eight months into her third pregnancy, and although we were scheduled to fly early the next week to a mission hospital—supposedly in plenty of time for the delivery—she was sure she had started labour.

This was one of those moments I had always dreaded when we first went to Papua. Of course, I had worried about Gloria or myself getting malaria or some other tropical disease. Probably my greatest concern, however, was about raising our children, giving them a proper education, and particularly about what to do in a medical crisis, where there was no doctor, clinic or hospital a phone call away.

People had wondered about our sanity, taking our firstborn son Jonathan with us from "civilized" Britain to live in the wilds of Irian Jaya. Some actually got quite angry with us and readily shared their opinions, which found their way back to us:

"Who do they think they are?"

"What kinds of parents are they, taking their infant son to such a primitive place? Have they no sense?"

"It is all very well that they want to serve God in the back of beyond among cannibals; but have they considered the dangers of raising their children in such a place?"

"Goodness knows what effects this kind of life will have on their children!"

Our simple rationale was that others had done it before. In my boyhood, missionary friends of my parents had stayed in our home with their kids and they had always seemed to be perfectly normal people. In anticipation of going to Papua we talked with other missionaries specifically about what they had done in regard to health and education and how their children had fared. What we saw and heard gave us the courage to believe that we could do it too.

It certainly wasn't easy, however. Soon after we arrived at Ninia, I was away with Bruno for a week hiking through the Seng Valley to participate in the first baptism of believers there. One day Gloria suddenly became aware that the house was unusually quiet. Jonathan, who was about two-and-a-half, wasn't making the usual play noises and Gloria went to investigate. She found him sitting on our bed chewing some pinkish pills.

I had placed a medicine cabinet fairly high up on the wall in our bedroom, but Jonathan had dragged a small, rickety rattan table across the room, climbed up onto it, reached into the cabinet and helped himself. Whether by accident or choice, he had taken out the bottle of flavoured infant Camoquin—antimalarial medicine—and stuffed a few in his mouth.

Thrusting her fingers firmly between his teeth Gloria felt inside his mouth and pulled out as much as she could, but there was no way of knowing how large a dose he had consumed. She picked him up and carried him over to the de Leeuw house where Marlys, a nurse, induced vomiting. It was too late in the day to call a doctor on the radio, and all they could do was pray and wait till morning. When they did get hold of a doctor, she assured them they had done as much as they could. Although she was prepared to fly in by mission plane, the wet, foggy weather meant there was no hope of that. There was nothing more to do but wait and pray, and slowly he recovered.

☙

Malcolm, our middle son, had been delivered safely at a Baptist mission hospital, and when we brought him back to Ninia, a number of young girls instantly volunteered to help look after him. It was customary for adolescent Yali girls to remain in the village to care communally for their younger siblings while their mothers went off to plant or weed their garden plots and harvest sweet potatoes. So it was the most natural thing in the world for them to assume that we needed a girl to look after Malcolm. It seemed a good idea, since it would free Gloria up to learn the language while managing a home without running water, electricity or other modern conveniences.

Kombukele—a short Yali girl, about twelve years old, with bright eyes and an engaging white-toothed smile—was appointed as child minder. At her request, we purchased a suitable woven string bag so she could carry him around suspended from her forehead and down her back, exactly like all Yali mothers do. The Yali women lined their net bags with leaves which could be easily changed when their babies did what babies do, but Malcolm's bag was lined with a small blanket.

He became so accustomed to this arrangement that he would crawl into the bag of his own accord if it was left on the floor, and if it was hanging on a nail, he begged to be put into it when he wanted a nap. Malcolm flourished with this easy life, well cared for at home and by the Yali children. But one day, we could see he was in distress and when we examined him, we noticed he had a painful swelling in his groin.

By shortwave radio we contacted Dr. Rob White, who had delivered him, and on his advice arranged a mission flight to take Gloria and Malcolm to the hospital. It turned out Malcolm had an inguinal hernia which the doctor was reluctant to deal with at the bush hospital. In the end, they were flown by MAF plane across the border into Papua New Guinea where Malcolm had surgery for the hernia. When they came home, crisis over, life soon returned to normal.

☙

Now, still at Ninia, we were expecting our third child, and Gloria was sure she had begun premature labour. Shaking me awake, she urged, "You better go and get Sheila." I slipped on some clothes, went out into the inky black of a starless, moonless night, ran along the stony path to Sheila's little wooden house and began pounding my fists on the door.

Sheila MacIntyre, a trained midwife from Scotland who had come to help at Ninia after the de Leeuws returned to Canada, reacted right away. "Go and put a kettle on and boil water to sterilize my equipment," she shouted through her bedroom window.

I was back in the house in a minute, moved the kettles to the hottest part of the stove, opened the damper and blew on the smouldering embers. In an instant the fire began to roar in the metal chimney and by the time Sheila came, one of the kettles was whistling. I poured the boiling water into the tray of obstetric instruments she had brought—just in time, because the baby was coming quickly.

As I stood looking over Sheila's shoulder, though, even my inexperienced eye could tell that the birth was not going to be straightforward. It wasn't the baby's head that started to show first, it was his tiny dimpled buttocks. Nevertheless, in an amazingly short time, the quietly competent nurse had deftly delivered Iain, our third son—her first breech birth! He was a tiny four-and-a-half pounds and just about four weeks premature. Of course we had no incubator, so we improvised with blankets and a hot water bottle.

After catching a short sleep, I rose before six a.m. to say goodbye to the evangelists who were about to head home. I stuck my head in the hut door where they had slept and now were eating a breakfast of sweet potatoes. "My friends, my son was born early this morning while you slept!"

One by one they popped excitedly through the doorway, like rabbits from their burrow, to hug and congratulate me—sharing my joy, and unaware how unnatural this birth had been for me!

ꕥ

It seemed no time at all before our three boys were away at MK[19] boarding school. It was customary for almost all the missionary children to attend a mission-run boarding school at Sentani on the north coast of Papua, and by that stage our three boys had three friends in the next valley. Art and Carol Clark and their sons had come from Canada and established their home in the Seng Valley, in the vast eastern part of the Yali area. So not only did we have new colleagues, but our sons had three new "cousins." Each semester the six boys travelled together by mission plane to the coastal school.

During their holidays in the village, our three enjoyed life to the full, running around with their Yali friends, exploring in the bush and climbing trees. They stalked crickets and katydids with miniature bows and arrows, dammed up a stream to make a swimming hole, taught Yali kids how to hold a book and "read" pictures, and, as they got older, ventured further afield to learn from the Yalis how to hunt, fish and camp in leaf shelters.

---

19 MK stands for "missionary kid." Like TCK (third-culture kid) it not only characterizes the children of missionaries, but hints at a way of life—the phenomenon of living in two cultures but not necessarily belonging in either.

There were always mixed emotions on the day the plane came to take them back to school in Sentani. While there was the excited anticipation of going back to the coast to meet up again with their expatriate friends, there was also the bitterness of leaving behind this alternate life and saying goodbye to their Yali buddies.

"I'm not going back to school," Malcolm informed his mother one day when he saw her getting their clothes ready and sewing on name tags. This was indicative of the inner tension each of the boys had, living in two worlds. "No, I'm not going, but in case I do, remember to pack my things!"

The day of departure was also a sad day for us. It wasn't like leaving one's small child at the school gate or seeing him board a school bus, knowing that in the afternoon he would be back home again and the incessant chatter would start all over.

How many times did we stand beside the airstrip smiling through our tears as the boys waved through the window of the little Cessna? How often did we listen to the changing throb of the propeller as the pilot prepared for takeoff, then watch as the pilot released the brakes and the plane rattled down the gravel slope? We would wait while the red-and-white aircraft lifted into the sky and banked off into the valley, the noise reverberating off the cliffs, until it disappeared from sight behind the mountain. Only then would we plod silently back to the now too-quiet house. Somehow that day was usually frittered away in inconsequential things, since we were too distracted to concentrate on anything demanding such as literacy lesson preparation or Bible translation.

We kept in touch, of course. Each Sunday, their dorm parent ensured they wrote a letter home, and these were delivered to the Mission Aviation Fellowship base to be sorted and put into personal mailbags. It might be a week or two (and sometimes longer) before we got a plane; but we always had our letters ready for the possibility of an unexpected flight. Whenever there were scheduled flights, Gloria always baked their favourite cookies or some other treat to send in the mailbag with the pilot. And each semester, we took some vacation time in the mission's guesthouse at Sentani where the boys could join us and the family would be together for a while. Then we'd look forward to the summer holiday, or Christmas, to be all together again.

As soon as the plane landed, they clambered out, each eager to tell his story to Mum or Dad or share some excited news with a Yali friend. We'd go up to the house and they would drink homemade juice and munch on a slice of freshly baked cake while they talked nineteen to the dozen. Several weeks of catching up were crammed into minutes. Then they'd be off in their rooms unpacking and checking for some favourite toy or book, then suddenly they were out of doors with their friends until the next mealtime.

They were home again. Life was normal—at least, according to the customary way of life for missionary kids in Papua.

Jonathan, Malcolm and Iain growing up in two worlds

Generally speaking, the boys thought this was a great life, living in two worlds: the periodic life in a western context at school and the adventurous life among the Yali at Holuwon. It could have been a lot worse—we've all heard horrendous stories about boarding schools around the world. However, our family was not totally unscathed.

During one semester, tension flared up in the dorm between the dorm dad and the boys who (putting it mildly) sensed that they were not being treated fairly or with appropriate dignity. From our perspective, the man was not up to the task of dorm parenting, and things came to a head one day when one of our boys cried out to us in a letter home, "Get me out of here!"

We were faced with a dilemma: should we leave Holuwon and relocate to the coast, where we might be able to continue translating and make occasional teaching visits to the interior; or was it time to leave Papua altogether? We appealed to our field leadership team, and after what seemed to us a long and even painful process, the situation was eventually resolved when the dorm parent and his wife were replaced by a more suitable couple. Nevertheless, at the time, we all found it a bitter and unnecessarily hurtful experience that, perhaps more than anything else, nearly forced us to quit and return to the UK.

With the passage of years, our boys now look back and see the incident as only a small fragment of their boyhood which dims in significance in light of the many wonderful adventures, privileges and benefits they enjoyed growing up among the Yali and being educated by a team of dedicated teachers in a multinational school. They still have friends from those days and from both tribes—Yali and MK—and they continue to make friends and have even married cross-culturally.

Like so many "third-culture kids," they have become international in their worldview, interracially comfortable and able to adapt to new situations. They are also very knowledgeable about international affairs and world history, globally minded, ecologically aware, and sensitive to the marginalized, seeking justice at all times.

CHAPTER 14

Andrew Walls

I never dreamed I would have the opportunity to attend university. My school days had proved to me that I wasn't an academic, or even a student, and the possibility of later developing into a "mature student" had not appeared on the horizon of my hopes or dreams until the day in 1985 when I met Professor Andrew Walls at the University of Aberdeen.

I was introduced to him by a fellow RBMU missionary, Ken Scott, when we were in the Granite City to speak at a student conference. Ken was taking postgraduate courses there at the time, and he insisted I meet the professor, an unpretentious man with an endearing manner and kindly blue eyes, who immediately put me at ease. He evidently knew who I was; my colleague Ken had obviously told him something about me, but he surprised me by saying, "I have read some of your writings, John. Have you considered coming to study at the Centre?" Professor Walls, a world-renowned church historian and missiologist, was referring to the Centre for the Study of Christianity in the Non-Western World, which he had founded at Aberdeen a few years earlier.

"I would love to be able to come and study here," I replied, "but I don't have a first degree. I only have the diploma from the BTI in Glasgow and the diploma in theology from the University of London."

"Nevertheless," he encouraged me, "I've heard how you've studied and learned the Yali language and you're engaged in Bible translation. If you applied to come here, I would go to bat for you with the university senate. You see, I want practitioners coming here, not just academics!"

Soon after that conversation, with the encouragement of my father and the support of the RBMU leadership, I applied and was accepted, not at Aberdeen but at Edinburgh University's Faculty of Divinity. The Centre had been relocated to New College. In 1986 I began a research degree there, focusing on the role of written Scripture in an oral society.

Later, I heard it said of Andrew Walls that one of his chief characteristics was his delight in promoting the personal development and scholarship of others. That was certainly true for me, and there is no doubt in my mind that my encounter with Professor Walls was a turning point in my life. He saw that potential in me which I did not recognize in myself, and in a professional and fatherly way he guided and encouraged me on my journey of research and self-discovery.

Enormous resources were available to me at New College and nearby locations: the extensive theological library of the Faculty of Divinity, the main library of Edinburgh University, the abundant archives in the National Library of Scotland, and the unique and copious collection of books, pamphlets and papers in the library of the Centre itself. Here, in the Centre, Andrew Walls assigned me a reading table where each day I spent many undisturbed hours while most of my fellow students found cramped carrels in the crowded faculty reading room.

Above all, it was an inestimable privilege to be studying with this distinguished and highly respected scholar of church and mission history. I was the sole western student in a small but diverse and gifted group of young men and women from Brazil, Hong Kong, Korea, Myanmar, Nigeria, and Zambia. We participated in seminars together and looked forward to the days when Professor Walls convened a "meeting"—as he preferred to call them—around a large table in one of the seminar rooms. He had a history of heart trouble, and on his cardiologist's instructions had been losing weight, so he came into the room wearing ill-fitting trousers hitched up with a leather belt, a generous brown tweed jacket and a nondescript wool tie. He always carried a sheaf of folders bulging with dog-eared notes which he placed on the table—as if these were the necessary resources to which he would refer.

However, it was all in his head and his heart. Without referring to the thick stack in front of him, he would just start to talk from the wealth of his knowledge and his deep personal reflections on the serial expansion of the church throughout history. He expounded on the conversion of societies to Christ in terms of the embodiment of the Christian faith within the particulars of a culture, what he called the "indigenizing" principle. He emphasized that "God in Christ takes people as they are" within their culture, so that the Christian faith becomes "a place to feel at home." He also stressed, nonetheless, what he called the "pilgrim" principle: the gospel gives people a new perspective on their own societies and orients them outwards to a new set of relationships, generating within them an awareness that here there is no abiding city or culture.

I took abundant notes, but it was impossible to keep pace with the fascinating teaching, peppered with anecdotes, references to other scholars, and original aphorisms which distilled his copious knowledge and profound insights. In the library I searched for and devoured every article he had written in his inimitable and erudite style, and what I read reinforced and complemented what I learned in "the meetings." It was only in retrospect that I discovered how much I had absorbed by a kind of cognitive osmosis as, day after day, I was exposed to this man with such scope of knowledge and astute perception.

The degree program consisted of continual assessment through participation in seminars and classes, a number of research papers on aspects of Christianity in the non-western world, and a final dissertation. There were no examinations as such, but external examiners (scholars as prestigious as Walls himself) read and critiqued our essays and dissertations.

I attended lectures and seminars taught by other distinguished professors and guest lecturers in addition to Andrew Walls. Among these was Kwame Bediako, one of Africa's foremost theologians—a Ghanaian.[20] His lectures were open to the public, and at the end of the final one he invited us to stand while he closed with an African prayer "from the rainforest." Instead of an eruption of applause at the end of a brilliant series of lectures, everyone remained standing in reverent silence for a few seconds, broken at last by tentative clapping which swelled into a worthy standing ovation.

The classes and the reading not only filled me with fresh knowledge and ideas, but stimulated me to think theologically and missiologically. Moreover, through my assigned and elective studies, I discovered in myself a latent appetite and talent for reading and research. Initially I was daunted when I saw the extent of my first list of reading assignments, and wondered out loud if this was recommended or required reading. I really doubted that anyone could read this amount of literature in the time available. However, once I got into a good mode of reading and note-taking, I employed every available moment and gradually expanded my reading. I spent many hours in the various libraries tracking down

20 Dr. Bediako was rector of the Akrofi-Christaller Institute for Theology, Mission, and Culture, in Akropong, Ghana. He died following a serious illness on June 10, 2008.

old out-of-print books and studying original documents brought to me in a tray from the archives. Every evening at home I spent another three to four hours reading or writing. People who have only come to know me in the last few years presume I have always been an avid student, but this is not so.

Even so, I came within a hairsbreadth of quitting within a week or two of starting this course of study. For one thing, I felt quite out of my depth. Around me were youngsters in their late teens and early twenties, and the few mature students I encountered were generally people with several degrees under their belts. I was at the front end of a steep learning curve and I did not have the confidence that I was up to the task.

The other matter that nearly scuppered me was finances. As a supported missionary I did not have adequate means, and to make matters more complicated, the mission was in tight financial straits and had just cut our living allowance by fifty percent. I did not see how we could pay the rent and buy groceries, let alone write cheques for the amount of the university fees. One day, I accosted Professor Walls on the way to his office, planning to give him my two reasons for quitting. "I am rather busy today, John. Let's have a wee chat tomorrow," he said.

The next morning in my Bible reading I came across the words in Psalm 37 where David, after complaining—as we all do—about how the wicked and powerful prosper, then asserts, "I was young and now I am old, yet I have never seen the righteous forsaken or their children begging bread."[21]

After breakfast it was our habit to read a few verses of Scripture and pray before the boys went off to school. I explained our financial situation and told them how these verses reminded me that God takes care of us and that somehow, he would meet our need. That evening, however, I trudged back despondently across the city as was my custom, to save every penny by not taking the bus even when it poured with rain. I was weighed down by a heavy bag of books on my shoulder and a burden of doubts and fears in my heart.

When I entered the flat, Gloria greeted me warmly and showed me two business envelopes addressed to me which she had left unopened. One was from an acquaintance who had enclosed a cheque for a sizeable amount of money. He knew the family would have needs—grocery bills, clothes for growing boys. "Just use the money as you see fit!"

The other came from the Jerusalem Trust. I had almost forgotten that the mission director had applied to this trust on my behalf, requesting a grant towards the cost of my studies. I had hoped that whatever they might give would at least alleviate the burden of the fees, but I was surprised to see the amount: a full grant with a simple obligation to acknowledge their help and the hope that

21 Author's paraphrase, Psalm 37:25.

the fruits of my studies would further the work of the ministry of the gospel.

The "children of the righteous" would not be begging for bread!

The following day I sat down opposite Professor Walls in his office. Books were stacked on the floor and his desk, not to mention those on the shelves lining the walls. His wife Doreen would eventually help him organize and archive these. She was cataloguing and organizing the Centre's vast resources that had recently been shipped from Aberdeen. It was clearly the office of a bookish professor! He looked at me over the top of his glasses with his kindly blue eyes and asked, "What is it you wanted to talk about, John?"

"Well, I had been planning to tell you I felt I should quit."

"It sounds as if you're having second thoughts," he responded hopefully.

I explained to him the double pressure I had felt, and that since God had removed the one obstacle, I presumed he would also enable me to persist in the course of studies even though I felt out of my depth. I don't recall now what Walls said to me, but I do know it was encouraging, and I walked out of his office without regrets and feeling empowered to begin in earnest my rigorous journey of discovery.

In July 1988 I received word that I had met the university's requirements with the submission of my dissertation, "Scripture in an Oral Culture: The Yali of Irian Jaya," and I was to be awarded the degree of Master of Theology. Since I was now back in Irian Jaya, I would graduate in absentia. My only regret was that my father could not share in my joy; he had passed away suddenly a few days earlier. Admitted into hospital with advanced cancer of the gall bladder, he quickly went into a coma after saying farewell to family members at home. It was a great shock for me to receive the news a few days *after* the funeral, when a telegram from my mother was read to us over the shortwave radio. It gave brief details and concluded, "Don't come home. You are doing the Lord's work."

This seemed typical of my stoical mother, but I was surprised by grief. My father's sister had passed away just before we returned to Irian Jaya from my study leave, and when I saw my dad at the funeral, I had wondered if I would see him again. Ironically, just a few days after the telegram brought its sad news of his death, I received a last letter from him written on a Sunday.

He had just preached in a vacant church on the Isle of Skye. "This morning I preached in Struan, where I am the interim moderator," he wrote, then, in understatement, "However, I have not been feeling very well lately and am constantly tired. Tomorrow I will go into Portree to see the doctor."

He was eighty-six years old and still surprisingly active. He hadn't known he was dying of cancer—or if he had, he had said nothing—but had continued to live a very full life. In one sense, there was no sorrow; but it was a cruel blow to hear the news in this abrupt way, so far from home, unable to join my family at the funeral and not present to share in the celebration of his life.

In retrospect, I am glad to have been surprised by grief. It is natural for me to think rationally about these things based on my knowledge of my father, his sound faith and his life, good and productive to the end. I accepted the certainty that he was in a "better place" and had "entered into his reward," as my mother put it when she wrote. I could give mental assent to the belief that we do not need to grieve as those who do not have the Christian's hope; and yet I was surprised by the invasion of grief beyond the protective fences of knowledge, faith and hope.

Nevertheless, though deeply disappointed that my dad had not lived to see me graduate, I live in the memory that he wholeheartedly encouraged me to pursue my studies and fully approved of what I was doing. He would have been thrilled if he had ever met or listened to Andrew Walls, and he would have been excited to see how I sought to apply what I had learned in Edinburgh to teaching and translating the message for the oral Yali culture.

CHAPTER 15

Forces for Change

For countless generations the Yali people had lived in protective yet inhibiting isolation within the remote ruggedness of the Jayawijaya highlands of Papua. This extreme seclusion meant, on the one hand, that their culture developed with unique and distinct characteristics: beliefs, values, social structures, language and ways of coping with life. On the other, it prevented the free intercourse with other societies through which the benefits of other people's knowledge, ideas and innovative solutions may be evaluated, tested and, if necessary or suitable, adapted and integrated into their own cultural system.

One anthropologist with experience in Papua New Guinea defined culture this way:

Culture is a more or less integrated system of knowledge, values and feelings that people use to define their reality (worldview), interpret their experiences and generate appropriate strategies for living; a system that people learn from other people around them and share with other people in a social setting; a system that people use to adapt to their spiritual, social, and physical environments; and a system that people use to innovate in order to change themselves as their environments change. [22]

Obviously, the Yali world and worldview began to change the day two foreign missionaries, Stan and Bruno, walked into the Heluk Valley.

Actually, the harbingers of change predated the arrival of the two men, one Australian, the other Dutch. I am sure we could trace back through history the steps that brought about this particular event, all the way back to Jesus when he told his disciples to go into all the world and make disciples from every ethnic group in ever-widening circles from Jerusalem through Judea and Samaria to the ends of the earth. And I recall one day when I stood on a lonely ridge where the mountains plunged to the southern plain of New Guinea and looked towards tropical rainforest stretching as far as the eye could see until it disappeared in a blue haze where sky and land merged, and thought, "This *is* the end of the earth!"

Long before Jesus's mandate, though, and without the constraints of his love that compelled his disciples twenty centuries ago to begin to push the boundaries outward from the heart of Israel and Judaism, human beings had already explored new frontiers and migrated across the face of the earth. There is a natural human

---

22 Michael Rynkiewich, *Soul, Self, and Society: A Postmodern Anthropology for Mission in a Postcolonial World,* Cascade Books, Oregon. 2011:19.

compulsion to climb a mountain, cross a river or ocean, venture beyond a divide and discover who and what lies beyond, that predates by far the outward-bound momentum of Christianity.

It started the day Adam and Eve left Eden. It picked up pace when Cain, having killed his brother Abel, became a "wanderer and fugitive" on the earth. It was still happening generations later when migrating peoples arrived in the Euphrates Basin and resolved together to build a ziggurat at Babel, and it was exemplified in the pilgrimages of Abraham through the Fertile Crescent into Canaan, then to Egypt and back again.

From time immemorial, people have migrated, both voluntarily and under duress, in search of land to call their own. They migrate to seek fresh opportunity, to make discoveries or to trade and interact with peoples unlike themselves. According to anthropologists, the peoples of New Guinea are where they are because of great migrations from Africa and Asia tens of thousands of years ago, and some degree of migration within Papua has continued into recent days.

New Guinea, "the last unknown," attracted not only these early voyagers, ancestors of today's inhabitants of Papua, but modern-day migrants, nomads, explorers, entrepreneurs and adventure seekers. In the last thirty years there has been an influx of transients and settlers, tourists and geologists, traders and profiteers, government officials, development workers and missionaries. In addition, modern communications, transport and economic development have suddenly thrust the province from the Stone Age into the technological one and even the age of electronic media.

One day as I walked through the highland town of Wamena I saw for the first time a telecommunications dish pointed toward the ether to receive microwave signals from across Indonesia and around the world. Meanwhile, a Dani man in traditional attire with an axe over his bare shoulder and a bow and arrows in his hand, strutted by nonchalantly, unaware of what it signified. Two distinctly different worlds were now perforce meeting in Papua.

In 1991, towards the end of the Gulf War, I flew from London to Papua. My flight from Britain, which was more than half empty, was diverted over Russia rather than the normal route across the Mediterranean and down through the Gulf to Asia. By the time I arrived in Holuwon, I had been out of touch with news media for days. When a Yali there asked me for news of the Iraq war, I found he was more up to date than I was. He had just returned the day before from Wamena where he had watched live military action on satellite TV!

The encounter between Papuans and the outside world has brought both bane and blessing. From the perspective of Papuans who are increasingly cognizant of the wider affairs of the world, the Indonesian government, through culturally insensitive officials, military and police, has at times been heavy-handed and even brutal, treating Papuans as inferior creatures rather than fellow citizens. Papuans feel robbed by international conglomerates who, with government permission and cooperation, invade and exploit the land they inherited from their ancestors. Wealthy western tourists—ostensibly there to observe the culture and learn from them—have often been insensitive, arrogant and selfishly exploitive.

Now Papuans have learned to their sorrow that sexually promiscuous tourists and officials have been the bearers of venereal disease and HIV/AIDS. In the last thirty years they have witnessed a huge influx of Indonesian government officials and "transmigrants"[23] into their province, to the point that immigrant Muslims now outnumber the native population and Islamic fundamentalists and militants associated with groups like Jemaah Islamiyah threaten their security. The demographic and socioeconomic conditions in Papua are going through momentous change.

Sadly, we selfish and insensitive human beings are too often the cause of adversity, exploitation and suffering, but the physical environment also causes hardships. While we lived among the Yali we shared in their experience of some of those natural disasters which are to be expected in that part of the tropics—the islands on the "ring of fire" in the southern Pacific, a mere four degrees south of the equator. We eventually concluded that we could

23 "Transmigration" was an official policy of the Indonesian government by which large numbers of western Indonesians were helped to settle in Papua.

count on a severe earthquake every seven years or so. There were three in the Yali area during the twenty years we lived in Papua.

Living among the Yali in Papua we were also subject to the effects of the tropical climate and diseases. Once, some people asked me what the most dangerous wild animal in Papua was, and when I replied, "The mosquito," they just laughed, thinking I was joking. However, the tiny mosquito is responsible for more sickness and death than anything else in Papua, and all the family except Jonathan succumbed to malaria at some time or other. In my case I had one very bad bout which was treated locally, but Gloria and our boys Malcolm and Iain also had it while away from Papua and were admitted to hospital.

One of our young Yali friends, Musa—probably still a teenager at the time—collapsed, unconscious, on the path while walking to the village literacy class one day. We talked by shortwave radio to Dr. Vriend in the Wamena hospital about his case. He urged us to fly him out to the hospital, but since the weather had been so bad for several days there was no hope of a plane coming in. We treated him with injectable quinine, but after three or four days he remained in a coma, so I called the Dutch doctor again. "Clearly he has cerebral malaria," he explained. "You have to get him out of the village and send him to hospital."

"But we've been shut in with fog and rain since I last talked to you, and there doesn't seem to be any prospect of a change in the weather," I explained. Sometimes, between May and August, when the southern monsoons pushed up against the mountains, the Holuwon plateau was completely blanketed with fog for weeks on end.

"In that case, I want you to open your emergency medical kit and give him an injection of phenobarbitone. We have to get the brain inflammation down. But, John, talk to MAF and get a pilot to stand by. This is an emergency!"

One of the pilots overheard the conversation and broke in. "I'll come down and wait at the nearest open airstrip, and if a window opens up in the fog, call me right away. I'll do my best to get in to Holuwon."

I went across to the hut where Musa lay unconscious. One of the elders and a friend were with him. "There's no change," they said. "He has never regained consciousness, but we have kept putting water into his mouth."

I explained what the doctor had said and told them, "We have to be ready to carry Musa to the airstrip as soon as we know a plane is coming. I am going to give him an injection to try to bring down the inflammation in his brain, but first, let's pray."

We laid our hands on him and I led in prayer. I don't remember exactly what I prayed, but as soon as we said "amen," Musa sat up, and as if just awaking from sleep, asked, "What's going on?" He couldn't believe he had been unconscious for days. I didn't give the injection, but reported back to the doctor who agreed we could cancel the flight.

Musa made a complete recovery, went to Bible school, got married, raised children, and taught in a Bible school. He recently completed a term in office as district president of the Holuwon churches. When we heard, via shortwave radio, that my father had passed away, it was Musa who came to my house, Bible in hand, to pray with me and bring God's comfort.

Not only tropical diseases bring stresses for the Yali. As subsistence horticulturalists they are susceptible to the vicissitudes of the tropical climate, such as the prolonged season of unceasing rain and fog, which results from the southern monsoon. It saturates the soil, making it impossible to plant, and sometimes leads to landslides which can wipe away someone's livelihood in one fell swoop.

On one occasion some of my friends asked me why I thought the sweet-potato leaves were getting "burned." The first time they asked me, they were referring to a new area that had recently been dug and planted, and they wondered if there was a poison in the soil that was causing the burning. One day a couple of weeks later when I went out for a walk, though, I saw it for myself.

The problem was much more widespread than I had understood, and I suspected it was even more serious, so I arranged for an Aussie missionary colleague and agriculturalist, Frank Tucker, to come to Holuwon. We chartered the MAF helicopter in order to take him on a survey tour around the area. As soon as he saw the situation he confirmed that it was potato blight, and our investigation determined that it had spread through every sweet-potato garden area between seven hundred and fifteen hundred meters above sea level, effectively impacting the entire population of the thirteen villages in the Holuwon area.

The prognosis was that this crop of sweet potatoes would fail, and within about six months the people would have nothing to eat but a few other less nutritious root crops like cassava and taro. Frank and I submitted a report to the Department of Agriculture and a few days later the head of the department called me to the provincial capital Jayapura to talk about the situation and discuss what they could do to help.

"Obviously, Pak John," he said with typical Indonesian respect, "in the West you would do aerial spraying, but we don't have the resources to do that at all, never mind over such a wide area. What do you think we can do for you?"

"I was wondering, sir, if you could provide us with seeds for alternate crops like sweet corn, beans, peanuts and soybeans, which they could plant among the surviving sweet potatoes. Then, even if the sweet potatoes are only the size of a little finger, they could at least feed them to the pigs, but the corn, beans and peanuts would keep the people alive and healthy."

"We can certainly provide those, Pak John, and also some other native Indonesian vegetables which might help them through this crisis, but how would we get them to Holuwon?"

"Sir, if you can provide four hundred kilograms of seeds, one Cessna plane load, and deliver them to MAF at Sentani, I will arrange for a direct flight to Holuwon."

With this amicable arrangement, we managed to get the seeds into Holuwon and, with the help of our church elders, distributed proportionately to each family in every village. In the end, disaster was not only averted, the crisis proved a blessing, because now everyone was committed to growing crops like peanuts and soybeans in addition to their traditional crops.

There were other occasions when food was in short supply for the Yali. When El Niño caused the great Australian drought in 1985, no one we knew in the western world had even heard of the phenomenon, but that year we saw and felt its impact in Papua. Every stream on the Holuwon plateau dried up, and the little spring into which we tapped for our water supply was reduced to a trickle—about one litre an hour. With our boys home, showers to take and laundry to do, it came to the point where we started to walk twenty minutes to a stream whose spring was high in the rainforest. What was more serious, though, was the subsequent food shortage for the Yali people.

One evening as we walked through the village, Gloria and I stopped to talk with the boys in what we nicknamed "the YMCA"—a hut of young unmarried Christian men. They sat around a large cooking pot supping a slimy green soup made from boiled sweet-potato leaves, spiced with a forest herb. It was all they had to eat that day.

It grieved us that we had enough to eat. We regularly purchased and brought in things like sugar, flour, powdered milk and canned goods, so we were able to make bread and had other ways of supplementing our diet when local produce was unavailable. Nevertheless, seeing the Yali folk reduced to such a meagre diet made us unconsciously cut back on what we were eating, and we actually lost some weight. Once again, however, with an appeal to the government and the support of people outside the country, we were able to obtain rice, canned fish and cooking oil which we could give away or sell at a token price so that hunger was staved off and people could keep going till the crisis was past.

We imagined the hardship and suffering these people had endured in former days; but even in the midst of the negative influences that were now insidiously creeping in, we saw things were also changing slowly for the better. Not only had intratribal fighting long ceased, the general quality of life had improved as malnutrition had all but disappeared. Goitre, once endemic, had been eradicated; the incidence of malaria had been reduced as manmade breeding grounds were drained; better health resulted from better nutrition through teaching and the introduction of additional crops like peanuts and soybeans. Children were now healthy and happy, and so were their parents.

The Yali attributed much of this to the acceptance of the gospel and their faith in God. One outstanding example of this centered on *sak,* the red fruit of a type of pandanus tree, known to be rich in vitamins and omega-3 fatty acids. In the pre-gospel era, women and children weren't allowed to eat this food because of a strict taboo rooted in an ancient myth passed down by the ancestors.

When the gospel was accepted taboos like this were quickly abolished, and in this case, the fact that women and children could now eat this nutritious fruit made a huge difference. But that was not all. One day some of the village elders told me that *sak* had formerly only borne fruit during a short season following the summer rains in January, but once the taboo was broken, the fruit-bearing season had expanded, and in some cases trees were bearing fruit well into the year, out of season.

How do you explain something like that? The Yali people of Holuwon knew the answer: "God has blessed us because we turned from walking in darkness in the old ways passed down by the ancestors, and now are walking in the light of the gospel."

CHAPTER 16

Written Scripture in an Oral Culture

The anomaly was not obvious to me at first. Like generations of Protestant missionaries before me, I had assumed that Yali Christians should have God's Word available to them, written in their own language so they could read it for themselves. It did not strike me as odd that I was intent on giving *written* Scriptures to people of an *oral* culture, whose knowledge, history and sacred lore were passed on by word of mouth in myth, legends, fairy tales, poetry and songs.

I simply wanted to be able to teach from any part of the Bible, and that meant someone needed to translate it. If no one else was available to do it, then I supposed I had to do it myself; and that meant putting it in writing and then teaching people how to read it!

Stan Dale had completed an initial draft of the Gospel of Mark before he was killed, and his widow Pat typed and mimeographed the manuscript to leave in the hands of the handful of Yali believers. Then Bruno, working with bilinguals like Luliap, began to make rough translations of portions of the Scriptures which were already available in the Dani language. They had completed draft translations of the Gospel of John and the Epistles of John and Philippians. In fact, I had used their work to help me in my study of the Yali language. However, these Scripture portions reflected the Dani idiom more than the Yali, and I was beginning to discover that there were significant grammatical differences. I needed more appropriate choices of expressions and key terms, and in the end, I decided to try my own hand at translation.

One day in the course of my initial attempts, I suddenly realized what seemed to be a major problem with tense usage in Stan's translation of Mark's Gospel. By that time, I had completed a basic analysis of the Yali language and written a description of the verb system with its different classes and tenses. However, I hesitated to make any radical changes without raising the issue first with Dr. Myron Bromley, a brilliant American linguist working in a nearby tribe and an honorary translations consultant with the United Bible Societies.

The Yali language of the Heluk Valley has three basic past tenses which can be described simply as 1) "today's past," used for anything which happened from daybreak until the time of speaking; 2) the "ordinary past," used from yesterday back through two or maybe three generations; and 3) the "remote past," only used to speak of the ancestral and mythical past. What was important to note was that this tense denoted a past for which there were no surviving eyewitnesses. There was no one who could say, "I was there," or even, "I heard my grandfather say that he saw such-and-such."

Stan had used this remote past tense in translating the Gospel of Mark, and it seemed that the people could not appreciate that the gospel was an *eyewitness* account. They could not see that Mark was writing about a Jesus or disciples whom he knew personally. Rather, they considered the gospel to be about a mythical person and a legendary time.

The significance of this became clear one day when we had a Canadian visitor who wanted to buy some bows and arrows from the people to take home as souvenirs. When he opened his wallet to extract some Indonesian rupiahs, one eagle-eyed salesman noticed other kinds of paper money. These had to be shown and their value explained: US dollars, Canadian dollars and Israeli shekels. "From Israel?" one man queried with evident excitement.

"Yes," I translated. "Our visitor travelled through Israel and visited the places where Jesus walked—Jerusalem, Nazareth and Galilee…"

I was immediately interrupted. "You mean Israel is a *real* place on earth and Jesus *really* lived there? You must get your friend to show this money and tell his story at the church service on Sunday."

In due course, I met with the linguist Myron Bromley, Siegfried Zöllner—a German missionary with many years of experience among the northern Yali people who lived on the other side of the central ranges—and two native Yali speakers, one from the north and one from the south. The consultation not only confirmed my findings, but together we identified other significant differences between the southern Yali language of the Heluk Valley and the related northern Yali dialects on the other side of the mountain range. I also took the opportunity to show Myron and Siegfried some of my own translation attempts, and the end result was that Myron, in his capacity as Bible Society translations consultant, recommended to my mission leadership that I be formally assigned to translate the New Testament into the southern Yali language.

I hoped to take translation training in the UK during my first furlough, but due to timing affected by our Indonesian visa renewal, it wasn't possible. Of necessity I did the next best thing: I bought books on translation principles and methods that I studied diligently on my own. In subsequent years, I was able to hone my skills further by participating in annual translators' workshops organized in Papua by the United Bible Societies.

As a teenager, I had enjoyed the dynamic paraphrase of the New Testament by J. B. Phillips. He wrote that a good translator should be able "to produce in the hearts and minds of his readers an effect equivalent to that produced by the author on his original readers."[24] That was what I wanted to be able to do.

The more I immersed myself in this task, the more I discovered the many challenges in the process of Bible translation to be overcome in order for its message to be dynamic, in the idiom of the people, and able to evoke the hoped-for response in their hearts. Sometimes the problem was simply that some things in the Bible had no equivalent in the Yali language. A typical example of this was the term "sheep"—an important feature in both the Old and New Testaments, but unknown to the Yali who lived in isolation in the interior of the island where no one had ever seen a sheep. Was it a viable option to substitute the word "pig"? The pig was the only common domesticated animal in New Guinea and was highly prized by the Yali people. For instance, in the parable of the Good Shepherd, could I use pig as the cultural equivalent of sheep?

One day I was looking for Salela, a scrawny, toothless man who ranked as a poor man among his fellow Yalis. "John, my father, Salela's pig did not come home last night," one of his friends enlightened me. "So he left early this morning to go and search for it."

---

24 J. B. Phillips, Preface to *The New Testament in Modern English for Schools*, Bles, 1959.

Much later, in the afternoon, I bumped into Salela who was on his way back into the village, leading his pig with a woven fiber tether tied around its foreleg. "I see you found your pig that was lost, my friend."

"Yes, my older brother. I tracked my pig all the way down off the plateau. He must have caught the scent of a wild sow, because he went all the way round from the Heluk Valley into the Balim Valley and I finally found him over here," he said, indicating a point diametrically opposite his starting point.

In the parable of the lost sheep, then, it would be quite meaningful to substitute "pig" for "sheep." Even a very rich Yali man might not own a hundred pigs, but clearly any man who lost one would go out and search diligently until he found it and brought it home. Nevertheless, in light of the Jewish abhorrence of pigs as unclean animals, the use of "pig" for "sheep" in this and other contexts in the Bible would certainly be improper. While in some instances a cultural substitute is acceptable, there are times when it is wholly inappropriate and would communicate the wrong meaning in translation.

Clearly you cannot say, for example, "Behold the piglet of God who takes away the sin of the world." In this case, we had to borrow the Indonesian word *domba,* and by showing pictures of sheep and talking about what they were like, we had to help them understand the characteristics of sheep. And—because the

Yali had their own categories of "clean" and "unclean"—they understood why the Jews would never sacrifice a pig.

We encountered other translation problems when seeking suitable terms for words like "angel" or "priest" or concepts such as "forgive" and "righteous." I remember wrestling over how to translate the verb "to bless" in the simple story where Jesus takes little children in his arms and blesses them. Enggiahap was working with me at the time and I asked him, "Can you tell me what the verb *wip-duruk* means?"

I already knew this verb meant "to curse," but what I was really asking him was how the Yali used the term, and what they believed happened when they uttered a curse. "This is what we do when we are perhaps angry with someone and we invoke a spirit by name or make an oath in the name of an ancestor to cause something bad to happen," he said. "Perhaps we curse their pigs so they will not be fertile, or their family, so a child will get sick or even die."

He then taught me two other words that each basically meant the same thing; in other words, they had *three* ways to curse someone. "What do you say when you want to cause good to happen to someone?" I asked naïvely.

"We don't have any word for that. That is not something we Yali people do," he explained laconically. The only way around this conundrum was to use a descriptive phrase, so we translated:

"Jesus took the children in his arms and asked God to cause good to happen to them."

The one issue I did not really address until near the completion of the New Testament was the implication of *written* Scripture for an *oral* culture. During my study leave at Edinburgh University, I explored the whole question of orality—the existence and use of oral skills and media among people like the Yali, in contrast to literacy and literary skills. It is not just a matter of literacy versus illiteracy. It is a matter of cultural predisposition, natural learning-style preferences, and how one transmits knowledge and traditions to the next generation.

Was I right to assume, then, that all, or even a majority of Yali people should learn to read? Was William Tyndale right in suggesting that even the man behind the plough could and should read the Bible for himself?

I discovered that many decades after the introduction of literacy and the printed Scriptures to tribal peoples in Africa, the number who could read and understand the Bible for themselves was very low. Was there, then, any alternative to the Bible as a printed book for people like the Yali? Could there be such a thing as an audio or oral Bible, and would that be appropriate?

God had indeed given us his Word in the form of written Scriptures. In fact, he had commanded and inspired the various authors to write the books and letters which constitute the Bible, and the priests and the king were instructed to make written copies of the Law for themselves. But clearly not everyone could read the ancient Scriptures, for we see that Ezra and the priests had to read them aloud to the Jews who returned from the Exile. And not only was it true in biblical times that the majority were hearers of the Word and not readers—from the times of the early church right up until the Reformation, most Christians were in the habit of listening to Scripture, not reading it for themselves.

What I hoped we could do was make the Bible as readable as possible, in such a way that when it was read aloud, listeners could understand it almost as naturally as the spoken word. To accomplish this, we deliberately included the features of the language which are normal and necessary to oral speech, but which are spontaneously omitted as redundant once people learn to read and write.

We also developed a literacy program which focused not only on the *reader's* apprehension of meaning, but on oral reading which the *listener* could understand as clearly as if the words on the page were spoken in regular conversation.

The result was amazing. I remember one Christmas when I asked a young girl of about twelve years of age to read part of the nativity story in Luke. Older men who were sometimes inattentive to Scripture reading sat up and leaned forward, their eyes riveted on the girl. They talked about it the next day: it wasn't just the fact that she read well, but that it sounded as if she was speaking to them!

At last, in 1992, the day came for the dedication of the Yali New Testament in a large, festive open-air ceremony. Someone had made a huge banner that was strung above the temporary podium. It stated in bold letters: "Today God speaks to me in my own language!"

CHAPTER 17

Earthquake!

A tectonic fault line runs right through the highlands of New Guinea, and whenever there was a shift in the plates, it wasn't unusual for us to feel tremors which shook and rattled our little wooden house and sent every Yali bounding outside with excited whoops and cries of "Earthquake!"

On one occasion we were sitting in the village yard for a pig feast when we all heard the ominous deep rumble and watched the earth roll towards us in slow motion and then pass under us like waves of the sea, the trees rocking back and forth like masted sailing ships at anchor. I wrote my dad, "We refer to the earth as *terra firma,* but an experience like that shows you it may be *terra,* but it is not *firma*!"

It's easy to joke about it when no harm is done, but on three occasions we saw the devastation and suffering it could cause. The most recent and closest to us happened in 1989. That day I was sitting with Luliap and Otto in our translation "office"—part of a storage shed by the airstrip—when a major earthquake struck.

I had never seen Luliap move so fast. It seemed to me that in one bound he leapt from his chair through the open door onto the airstrip. Otto and I were close behind. Opposite us a huge cloud of dust rose from a rockslide that still rumbled on the other side of the valley. We ran to the house to make sure everyone was OK and I turned on the radio to check with our missionary neighbours.

Sue Trenier, working among the Hupla people at Soba two valleys west of us, had been thrown off her feet by the initial jolt and just missed being buried underneath a large bookcase and its load of books when it keeled over in the violence of the first jolt. She was expecting a plane in a few minutes, so I suggested, "You better check the airstrip for damage."

She reported back, "There are three seemingly bottomless cracks in the middle of the landing strip, and we're also receiving reports of landslides and possible casualties in nearby villages." Even as we talked, there was a series of aftershocks and she ran outside till they subsided. When she came back on the radio, I urged her, "Set up the radio outside the house, take out some necessary supplies and find a safe place away from falling rocks and trees. In fact, her timber house had been shaken clear off its foundations, and a rockslide had come within a few meters of her back porch.

In the meantime, I called the main MAF base on the radio and asked them to despatch their two helicopters immediately so we could start search and rescue operations. I reported that the Soba airstrip was unsafe and there were casualties, but someone wanted to know who was authorizing my request and who would pay the bill. "Just send the choppers!" I replied with some exasperation. "This is a disaster—we'll figure out the funding later!"

As it happened, an English MAF pilot, David Marfleet, had been flying his Cessna 185 up the Balim Valley towards the MAF base at Wamena when the earthquake struck. He watched rocks and trees crashing down everywhere and clouds of dust from rockslides filling the air. One massive landslide had actually dammed the mighty Balim River. He called ahead to his colleague Mike Meeuwsi, "Get one of the choppers ready for me. As soon as I land, I'm coming back here to begin search and rescue." Mike had just completed maintenance on one of the helicopters, so he readied that one for David and then set about preparing the second one for himself.

When I finished speaking on the radio, I became aware of a woman's wail. "My boy, my son! He's up on the mountain with Jonathan and Malcolm. Are they safe? Have they been killed?" In the urgency of the moment I had forgotten that two of my sons and some of their Yali friends were on a hunting trip in the forest above Holuwon, but I had assumed that there was no major damage around us except from fragile rock faces and areas prone to landslides. Some of the men agreed with me that the boys would be safe since Yariut was with them. He knew how to survive by keeping to ridgelines and avoiding danger zones.

But I had no more time to think about them, because David was landing at Holuwon. He had been to Soba and offered to evacuate Sue, but she needed to stay and tend to the injured who were already being carried in. However, he had brought Sue's guest, who was heading home to England and had been waiting for the MAF plane when the quake hit.

As we flew into the Soba Valley we could see the devastation everywhere, and after checking with Sue and some of the Hupla leaders, we set out to search the area and rescue casualties, especially anyone stranded in a precarious situation. We landed at a narrow ridge-top village where huts stood all askew, teetering on the edge where a landslide had fallen away to the river below. A bloodstained Hupla man picked his way through the debris towards us carrying the crushed body of a young woman. "Don't worry about her," he told me in accented Yali. "Just take out the injured. I will lead those who can walk to safety."

Back and forth we flew, shuttling the casualties to the Soba airstrip where Sue and her Papuan assistant Regina were busy immobilizing broken limbs with splints, dressing wounds and bandaging bleeding heads. On one of our flights, David noticed two women and a child right in the middle of a huge mudslide. He was not able to land, so he held the chopper in a hover while I let myself down from the skid to the ground. Immediately I sank in up to my knees in the slurry, so I climbed back onto the skid and grabbed the headset I had left on the seat.

"Dave, you'll have to get someone to help me," I shouted above the chatter of the rotor. "The soil is like churned butter and if I lift anyone up, I'll just sink deeper into the mud."

Soba earthquake (1989): An entire garden area destroyed

As soon as I was back on the ground, he pulled the helicopter up and wheeled away towards Soba to fetch someone to help me. Carefully, I made my way through the rocks and mire towards the forlorn huddle of mud-bespattered women and a small child clinging, frightened, to each other. Once again the earth shook beneath us and an ominous rumble came from the mountain far above. I looked up in time to see a huge boulder the size of a garden shed tossed into the air. The perspective made it seem as if it would crash directly down on us, and I thought, *This is it*, but it smashed into the ground maybe five hundred metres away, sending up a spray of mud. Almost immediately there was a rushing wind, followed by an avalanche of mud. It tossed trees like matchsticks and filled the air with pellets of mud and small stones which rained down on us as it swept past like a rushing freight train. It was terrifying. I felt for these folk, stranded, injured in this mudslide, who had already endured two or more hours of this frightful terror. I had been here only minutes, but it felt like an eternity.

What a relief it was to hear the throb of the chopper's rotors above the perpetual noise around us. I was glad to see a Hupla lad I knew who spoke comprehensible Yali step gingerly down from the helicopter. Together we lifted the injured one by one and carried them as gently as we could through the mud. While David kept the chopper hovering as steadily as possible, we lifted each casualty into the cabin. The pilot had removed the seats and doors earlier to make this easier, and we just set them on the plywood floor and secured them with cargo straps for the short journey to safety and help.

At some point, Mike had arrived with the other helicopter, so while David went to Holuwon to refuel from supply drums, we went in search of other casualties. Not far from Soba on a precipitous hillside, we found a man whose femur had been crushed by a rolling boulder. It was not only too steep to land, it was quite dangerous to make a close approach as the rotor blade almost intersected with the line of the slope. Mike warned me to keep my movements as gentle as possible, and since the injured man understood Yali I could explain what I needed him to do.

"I will help you onto your good leg and you can support yourself on me. Wait till I give the word, and while I lift you, grab hold of the helicopter and haul yourself in. I will take care to guide your injured leg."

It must have been agony for him, and it was a scary moment for us all. Mike confessed afterwards, "That felt too close for comfort; I almost aborted because the rotor blade was inches from the slope!"

Sometime during that long morning, I got word that Jonathan, Malcolm and their Yali friends were safely back in Holuwon. That was a relief. I had been confident that Yariut would look after them, but there was the realistic fear of an incident beyond their control. In fact, if the quake had struck a few seconds earlier they would have been halfway across a rockslide area. As it was, rocks crashed down nearby and swaying trees, clashing together, catapulted large fruit and branches through the air. The young Yalis had dropped to the ground, crying out, "God, help us! Jesus, have mercy and save us!"

When the first tremors ceased, Yariut told them, "Be quiet! Let me think!" This was his hunting ground, and in his mind he held a virtual topographical map of the area. He outlined his plan to the boys: they could follow a series of ridges which would avoid any danger zones and reach the village of Yalisili, and from there continue down to Holuwon. "When I say stop, you all stop, and when I say run, everyone runs."

They ran! They ran and did not stop until they reached the village yard at Yalisili, where Jonathan set his camera on a tripod and took a group portrait. Exhaustion is etched onto every face in that memorable photo—the fatigue of physical exertion intensified by the weariness that sets in after an adrenalin rush and emotional strain.

By midday an MAF Cessna had landed at a safe strip near Soba, so Mike began shuttling the seriously injured for transfer to the hospital at Wamena, while Dave and I resumed the search and rescue. At the south end of the valley, far from any village, we found two men in a small clearing totally cut off by landslides and cliffs. One seemed uninjured, while the other had something wrong with his leg. In the middle of the clearing was a large flat slab of rock with a small tree beside it.

"Look, Dave," I said on the intercom, "If you can hover over that rock, I can hang from the skid and drop down with the axe and machete I brought. I'll get the able-bodied man to help me and we'll chop the tree down and cut back the undergrowth."

Dave agreed, so I climbed out onto the skid, tossed the axe and machete to the ground and dropped down onto the rock. It took the Hupla man only a few minutes to fell the tree while I cut back the scrub around the rock and we made the clearing safe for a landing. The men were relieved and sat, apparently unconcerned, on the floor of the chopper with nothing but a single cargo strap between them and the gaping void as Dave swung the helicopter out into the valley and we looked straight down at several hundred meters of vertical cliff.

As night approached, the pilots decided to return to Wamena and offered to take Sue and Regina with them. "No, we'll stay here with our patients," they told us. "We have food and blankets and we'll just stay in these huts by the airstrip."

I felt guilty as I rode in the helicopter with the pilots, knowing I would have a hot shower, a good meal, and a comfortable bed for the night. But I tossed and turned on the bed's water mattress so that every undulating movement became an echo of an earth tremor or evoked some awful recollection of the trauma of the day. I was glad when morning came and we could resume our activity to blot out my mind's incessant replay of those disturbing scenes.

By the end of the second day, thanks to more skilful flying manoeuvres by the two pilots, the search and rescue operation was finally complete. About 136 people were missing or dead—quite a toll for an area where population wasn't dense and there were no stone or concrete structures. Most of the casualties had occurred in and around Soba, and now all the injured had been transferred to hospital. Sue and Regina were flown to Holuwon. Soba was deserted.

Over the ensuing weeks we cooperated with the Indonesian government and international aid agencies to provide blankets, cooking pots, tarpaulins, food and clothing for the thousands of survivors. They had fled their villages and made camps on ridge tops high in the rainforest. Local church leaders showed tremendous initiative and compassion, organizing these refugee communities and ensuring that needs were met even-handedly whenever the helicopter came in with food and gifts. One interesting outcome was that some of the traditional chiefs lost their power of influence overnight because they were only interested in their own survival and acquiring goods. They failed to rise to the occasion, whereas the elders and pastors committed themselves to serving the people.

In time, as the area became more secure, without further threats of aftershocks, people began drifting back into the valley to rebuild homes, plant again, have babies and raise families. Grieving doesn't necessarily end, but life must go on.

In August 2009, the Hupla people invited Gloria and me back to Soba. As the MAF plane circled prior to landing, we could see that the earthquake scars on the landscape had healed and there was fresh growth where twenty years ago it had been barren. Some trees had been strategically planted and native vegetation had sprung up naturally in other areas. The whole valley seemed rejuvenated. When the plane taxied to the top of the sloping airstrip we could see a huge welcoming crowd: smartly dressed men, women with new, colourful net bags, flowers and other decorations on their heads, and scores of healthy-looking children.

We had thought we would just be in Soba for a church leaders' seminar and a ladies' retreat, but in *their* minds it was an occasion to remember the 1989 earthquake and give thanks for the healing God had granted the tribe and their homeland. It was also an opportunity to recall how the gospel had been brought to them and to express their thanks to us missionaries.

PART 3

CANADA (1991 TO THE PRESENT)

CHAPTER 18

On a Good Day

On a good day at Holuwon, it was hard to imagine ever going back to Scotland. Whenever I looked out over the village at the spectacular mountain range with its series of knife-edged limestone ridges and the varied green hues of lush rainforest, then turned to look down the wide V of the valley where the Balim River carved its way, unseen, through rocky canyons towards the lowlands, blue in the distance, a great sense of joy and satisfaction would wash through me.

I'd listen, distinguishing the familiar sounds: the quiet murmur of voices in the huts, the contented chatter and bubbling songs and laughter of children playing, the distinctive twitter of woodswallows swooping overhead, or the surprisingly raucous call of a small flock of Queen Carola's bird of paradise feeding in the treetops.

I would savour the lingering smell of woodsmoke from the morning fires, but sense it being carried away by the breeze now drifting up fresh and unpolluted from the dewy forest below.

Many a time my awareness of the unexpected privilege of living and working here among the Yali people caused me to choke up. I was doing something valuable and at the same time personally fulfilling, making friends with remarkable people from an exotic culture, doing a job with variety and an unpredictable routine. I couldn't imagine living in a cityscape among anonymous crowds, taking public transport to a nine-to-five office job day after day, doing something monotonous, unchallenging and of no great consequence. I didn't belittle the work so many had to do to turn the wheels that made urban life work, and which put bread on the table and paid the utility bills. It was simply that every now and again I paused and appreciated the opportunities, benefits and satisfaction of the job I believed God had given me to do.

And on a good day like that, I dreaded what would happen when it ended, which I knew it must. Sometimes I pictured the family living in some claustrophobic flat in a dingy, dreary stone tenement overlooking a narrow, busy street in Edinburgh. I could visualize myself looking out the drafty window at the cold drizzle falling unrelentingly from a grey overcast sky to wash the road with a wet sheen which reflected the drabness of the day. I imagined miserable people scuttling along in that damp drabness under black umbrellas tilted against the wind and spray while cars and buses swished by, heedless of the additional misery they left in their wake.

And what would I be doing there?

The answer slowly began to unfold in 1990 when, after almost twenty years in Papua, we returned to the UK, still unsure if we had come home for good or whether this was merely to be an interlude to allow our sons to complete high school and go on to university. Initially, it felt like other leaves, which we usually spent in rented accommodations in London, though our last time had been in Edinburgh. On those occasions we all felt like transients, not putting down roots and fearful of developing close friendships. It was an unreal existence, not like a vacation, because we still had duties and responsibilities to the mission and our boys had to enter the British school system. We all lacked a sense of purpose and meaning. It was like waiting at a bus stop, not knowing if the next bus would ever come, or if it did, whether it would be going where we wanted to go.

It sometimes felt lonely too. Friends from the past had moved on—some to other cities because of new employment opportunities, some in other ways, with new circles of friends and different interests. Not only had people moved, we found the entire British culture had gone through dramatic shifts in the years we had been in Papua. At first we couldn't have told you what it was, and most of our friends could not have named what had happened in the intervening years, but it was like a sea change. While we were devoting twenty years to a remote and fairly motionless cultural backwater in New Guinea, postmodernism, with all its profound philosophical, social, religious and political currents, had been transforming the contours of western life as we had known it.

But we had changed too. As a friend aptly stated it, we had drunk deeply from the well of a very different culture, and consequently our own worldview, with its tacit beliefs and suppositions, had been fundamentally challenged and transformed. We now felt "out of sync," not just chronologically but in other ways too, with our native culture. We had adopted a less materialistic mindset by moving far from the compulsions of western consumer society and living instead among subsistence horticulturalists. We had learned to question the individualistic values of post-Enlightenment culture while living face-to-face with a people who valued life in community. We had ceased to think in black-and-white dichotomies and distinctions between scientific thought and philosophy. Through our growing understanding and intercourse with our tribal friends, we had started to think more holistically. We no longer felt at home in Britain.

Added tension came from the fact that, though we had left Papua, I still had practical ties to the place. There was an ongoing project to complete the translation of the Bible which I was supporting at a distance and for which I would need to return periodically to help with checking and ensure it kept moving. Luliap Bahabol and Otto Kobak had been recognized as "mother-tongue" translators by the Indonesian Bible Society, but they still needed my help. I concluded that if I took a job in the UK, I would need the flexibility to take time out for four-to-six-week visits to Papua at least once and maybe twice a year.

Unexpectedly, a possible solution came to us. We had previously been asked if we would consider moving to Canada to help in our mission office there, but at that time, we were still too fully committed to completing the translation of the Yali New Testament. Now, however, with the manuscript already in the hands of the publishers, the invitation came again.

It was a tough decision, but after considerable prayer and discussion among our family and with the folks in Canada, we agreed to pack our bags yet again and cross the Atlantic. We had posed some conditions which happily proved acceptable: I was to be allowed to use part of my time for translation work, including necessary, periodic trips to Papua; and this was not to be a permanent assignment. It still left the door open for a return to Papua at a future date. Much also depended on our sons and their education.

It seemed to us a good arrangement, and in many regards it was, but it entailed major adjustments we had not anticipated. The sense of not feeling at home and being in some kind of limbo continued, now exacerbated by subtle and unexpected cultural adjustments.

Subconsciously, we had assumed that the move to Canada would be relatively easy. After all, we were experienced cross-cultural missionaries who had made the transition from British life to living among so-called Stone-Age people in Papua. Moreover, Canada was a former British colony where people spoke and wrote fairly British English, drank tea and were governed by a British-style parliamentary system. The similarities did prove to be there, but that made the subtle differences all the more significant.

We all found adjustment to life in Canada more stressful than we had imagined. Looking back, it was not simply a question of adapting to another culture, but also the lingering angst we felt on leaving what had been home to our family, the place two of our children had been born and where we had raised all of them over the previous twenty years. Instead of the land with its mountain vistas and lush, unspoiled tropical forests, we now lived in the unimaginative urban sprawl of flat and featureless southern Ontario.[25] Having lived in a face-to-face society where every person was appreciated for who they were, we now lived in a faceless society where people sought their identity in their jobs, where they lived, the kinds of cars they drove, and the style of clothes they wore.

In all honesty, pervading this was my own sense of loss of identity and purpose. The years in Papua had overall been very enjoyable, and the work varied, meaningful and productive. It had given me a great sense of self-worth. Now it began to feel as if I was slowly but surely sliding into a nebulous state of anonymity and obscurity, not sure any more who I was or what I should be doing. After having developed literacy materials, led a New

---

25 This is how we saw Ontario then. Having lived there much longer now, we have come to appreciate its beauty and its attractive small towns.

Testament translation project, taught and trained leaders, and in other ways helped establish a church, I now felt as if I was of no consequence—especially when I went to church.

The words of the song "On a Clear Day (You Can See Forever)" were written with the idea of prescience, the ability to see into the future and understand who you are and what you will accomplish. But the common experience is the opposite. All those times in Holuwon when I had anticipated leaving Papua and returning to the West, I had not imagined what would be involved in the transition. I knew there were "re-entry" seminars offered for children of missionaries to help them make the adjustment from living as third-culture kids in another land to life in the world of their parents. But no one seemed to have paid attention to the need for missionary parents to be helped in their adaptation to western culture when a lengthy overseas career came to an end. It took me a long time to process this. It was unanticipated. It was humbling.

CHAPTER 19

Necessary Change

Sometimes I felt dead.

Obviously, I was still physically alive. I was still breathing, I had a pulse, I continued to eat and drink, I went through the motions of work, social and church life, but now it was with a sense of numbness. I was in a Scots *dwam*—a vague dream or dull stupor. After moving to Canada I began to experience an unexpected range of emotions, from intense loneliness to deep-seated anger, frustration and a sense of worthlessness.

I had known some of these feelings before. Twenty-five years previously, when I had first moved from Scotland to live and work in London, I had experienced the same sense of loneliness. It had engulfed me one day while riding the crowded Underground. I remembered thinking, *Here I am, packed shoulder to shoulder in a train compartment in a city of ten million people, and yet I feel all alone.*

I also knew what anger was. In fact, a colleague had once courageously taken me to task for an unwarranted outburst. On another occasion, I had engaged in a heated altercation with one of my old Yali friends in the village who came to my door at nightfall and demanded I buy ten or fifteen kilograms of sweet potatoes from him. "Look, Hwenie, my friend," I'd said, "I don't need any more sweet potatoes. I already have a huge pile! Can't you see?"

As if he hadn't heard my plain logic, he repeated his imperative. "Buy my potatoes, my friend!" At that, my fuse blew, and I hoisted his bulging net bag of potatoes and tossed it angrily out of the house. "Take your potatoes and go," I had shouted after him. After I calmed down, I had mulled it over and felt quite ashamed, knowing I needed to make amends. The next day I had apologised to him publicly in church.

Regrettably, it was not the last time I had exploded with rage. Sad to say, I had often justified my anger to myself because the Yali people practised a kind of ritualized anger called "suahal." A plaintiff would stand in some prominent or central part of the village and vehemently verbalize his complaints to all and sundry so that people would take notice and step in to help resolve his grievance.

I did this myself once. Over a period of weeks or months, a single dog persistently broke into my tightly fenced duck pen and killed one bird after another. After the twenty-seventh (which happened to be significant number for the Yali), I marched into the middle of the village, armed with my black palm bow and a bunch of arrows, and there, at the top of my voice, I had called out, "If I ever catch a glimpse of that dog Sindulum, I'll put one of these arrows through him. He has killed off a full count of twenty-seven of my ducks!"

At that point, my friends had quickly stepped in to calm me down and assure me they would take care of things. Sure enough, they helped resolve the issue peacefully. The dog Sindulum was banished from the village and I was given a small pig in compensation.

Finally, I—like so many people—had struggled with self-esteem. Often my memory takes me back to my boyhood when Miss Sharpe unendingly nibbled away at my fragile ego with her unkind and demeaning words. She probably affected me as much by her failure to commend or encourage me for my achievements as she did by her unkind or careless criticisms.

In contrast, during my twenty years among the Yali people I had always felt accepted as a fellow human being. They stood up to me when I was wrong, supported me when I was right, and comforted me when I grieved. Unlike westerners, they did not find worth or identity in one's actions, dress or social status. Even the lowliest and least gifted among them were accepted just for who they were, not for what they did or possessed.

I recall a deaf-mute boy they called Apele. When his mother was pregnant with him, she suffered from goitre caused by endemic iodine deficiency, and her son displayed typical signs of cretinism. Besides being deaf, his head was an odd shape, his body was slightly deformed and stunted, and he walked with a strange gait. His given name had an ironic humour to it, because Apele means "a man's speech." But as he grew older, the Yali people renamed him Adam (a man), and everyone treated him with love and respect as a fellow human being, interacting with him through their own intuitive version of sign language.

Now, having moved to Canada, the full range of these feelings of loneliness, poor self-esteem and simmering anger had seeped insidiously out of my heart with renewed force and deeper significance. I remember one day saying to my wife Gloria, "I feel so alone; I have no friends here."

"What about Elmer? You like him." Elmer was the director of the mission in Canada, and we had met him a few times before we moved there.

"Yes, I do like him. He's very personable and I enjoy his company and his dry sense of humour, but he's not my friend yet." Generally, I found Canadians, at least those who lived in urban Ontario, courteous and friendly, but hard to get to know. In the stores, people greeted me warmly, much more so than I remembered back in Scotland, but it was anonymous and superficial.

Although there was a visible openness, with wide streets and unfenced front yards, it seemed hard to find a welcome into people's homes. It wasn't easy simply to drop by for an informal chat and a cup of tea or coffee; we discovered that such visits had to be planned in advance. Perhaps it was because busy urbanites didn't want to be caught unawares; the house had to be tidy and the hostess prepared. Even at church, although we found fellow immigrants welcoming, since we shared common experiences of cultural adjustment, the native Canadians and long-term residents seemed reluctant to go beyond formal friendliness.

In short, after living in Indonesia, where we had become accustomed to the open and accepting friendship of Papuan people and their deeply relational society, it was unsettling to be confronted with the cold individualism and frenetic busyness of Canadians whose friendships even had to be written into their schedules.

I had left a lot of close friends behind in Papua, not only Yalis, but also missionaries from America, Australia, Canada, Germany, Holland and elsewhere. We had developed deep bonds and camaraderie as we lived challenges, sorrows and exciting experiences together. However, it was not just the loss of a community of special friends, the kind with whom you argued, played, discussed and grieved, it was also the absence of familiar social landmarks, the lack of a sense of identity, the loss of a sense of place, the absence of a sense of belonging.

At that time, we were officially "resident aliens" in Canada, and sometimes I felt that that was the problem—we really *were* like aliens from another planet. Unlike other immigrants, we were oddities. We may have been English-speaking Caucasians, we were British, but we were somehow different, and no one seemed able to connect to us with our weird stories from a remote and unimaginable culture.

Apparently, I was also a little intimidating to some people in the church. When I confided to someone that I was frustrated that I had no opportunity for ministry, his response spoke volumes: "Don't you realize the pastor feels threatened by you? You have been a missionary, translated the Scriptures and trained church leaders. Who wouldn't feel threatened?" This revealed the other dimension of my feelings. I was not simply grieving the loss of friends or a ministry that had provided immense job satisfaction: I was also craving recognition and esteem. I wanted a sense of purpose and fulfilment, and through that, a clear identity in this new society where I found myself.

I remember one glorious winter's day we walked to church in sub-zero temperatures, the snow crunching and squeaking under our feet, the sun shining from a clear blue sky. It may have been midwinter in Canada, but who couldn't feel some joy on such a magnificent day with the sun glistening on pristine snow? It seemed to affect the congregation—they sang their hearts out—and the pastor too seemed at his best as he delivered an interesting and uplifting message.

When we got home to our little town house, as Gloria busied herself in the cramped kitchen preparing lunch, I stepped in to help, and in that instant the day changed. I don't even remember what was said, and it doesn't matter, but I snapped. I exploded.

A furious rage, frightening in its intensity, suddenly welled up in me, coursing through my veins and crowding out all reason and sensibility from my heart and mind. I had never experienced such unreasonable fury before. I remember shouting, but above all I recall the desire to smash things. I wanted to throw china dishes on the floor, toss chairs about, and even punch a hole through the wall.

I didn't, but I knew someone who had. One day in Papua, I saw a missionary friend with a cast on his hand, and I asked him if he had been in a motorbike accident. "I wish," he said. "No. I blew up at something insignificant that happened at home and put my fist through a wall."

At the time, I had thought it was funny, and we both laughed about it. But this wasn't funny. I was so enraged I knew if I didn't get out of the house, someone might get hurt, so I grabbed my parka and gloves and went out for a walk. I don't know how long I trudged the icy sidewalks, but as I walked I started what I thought would be a one-sided conversation with God: I would talk; he would listen.

"God, you know how I started this day rejoicing, and how much I enjoyed the service at church. Then I went home and started to help my wife. You saw what happened."

"Do you do well to be angry, John?" I didn't recognize immediately that this sounded a lot like the prophet Jonah's conversation when he was mad at God because the gourd that had been sheltering him suddenly shrivelled up.

"Yes, I do!" I snapped back. "I'm justified in being angry. I have every cause to be angry." I walked on in silence, still mulling over and over again what had happened that morning, still justifying myself and still blaming everybody and everything else. God did not interrupt me. He let me rant and rave in my heart until the steam of my anger had dissipated.

Finally, "Why are you angry?" It was then that I began to see more clearly some of the immediate causes of my pent-up frustration, disappointment and anger, but I dug deeper too. Although this was not by any means the first time I had exploded, it was the most intense and extreme instance, and I had been shocked by its depth and extent. Fundamentally, though, all anger has the same source: self. Self on the throne of my heart: the wounded self who has been hurt in the past and still carries grievances; the proud self who wants to make a name for himself; and the perfectionist self who loves to be right, always expecting too much from others and demanding too much from himself.

Twenty years previously, I had sat on a rock by the Heluk River, recalling the words of Jesus to his disciples, "If anyone would be my disciple, he must deny himself and take up his cross daily and follow me."[26]

Now, after all these years, I realized just how much more I had to learn about what "to deny myself" really meant. It meant saying no to the god in my heart who is me. Like all human beings, I like to be in control, and when things get out of hand, or when I, as king of my life, am threatened, I get angry. I like to be right and see things done right. While I love a degree of freedom or flexibility, I want to bring structure and order into my life and the lives of others. I like to have a specific role which matches my abilities so I can excel. I love to have a clear sense of personal identity and be esteemed for my successes and achievements. I had experienced all these things by the time we left Papua, but now everything seemed to have been taken away.

"So what are you going to do about your anger?" The Holy Spirit had been listening all along, and now he probed my heart.

I knew the answer. "There is nothing I can do! I need you to rip out the selfish, secret roots of anger in my heart, and only *you* can change me. I know I am personally responsible for my sin, but there is never anything I can do about it." In a cooler and humbler frame of mind, I headed home to the family.

---

26 Author's paraphrase, Luke 9:23.

Some years later, I was apologizing to one of my sons about something—I don't even remember what it was. I told him I was sorry for all the times I had been angry with him and his brothers. "Yes, I know, Dad, you were often angry like that, but you have changed," he said.

Yes, by God's grace, we *can* change.

CHAPTER 20

Living Between Worlds

The dugout canoe, powered by a small outboard, seemed to glide with the current as we made our way northwards between green walls of virgin forest. It was early in the morning as we followed the meandering course of the Tapanahoni River in southern Suriname, not far from the border with Brazil. The bright sun beat down, first on our left, then our right, as we rounded one bend after another. Above the gentle sputtering of the motor and the gurgle of water along the hull of the canoe, I heard the squawking of a pair of scarlet macaws, the unfamiliar calls of unseen jungle birds, and the twittering of swifts and swallows that swept low and systematically across the water in search of insects. At each new reach of the river, a blizzard of migrating yellow butterflies crossed our path, all heading unsteadily eastwards towards French Guiana.

I had come to Suriname a few days earlier to travel with Roy Lytle, a seasoned missionary who had spent over twenty years among the Wayana Indians. Roy was nearing retirement and the mission wanted my help in evaluating the ministry and the maturity of the church among two groups of Amerindian peoples strung out on two separate river systems in the southern rainforest. These people live far from the nation's capital, speak their own distinct languages, and are still largely untouched by civilization. In some respects, it was like being back in Papua, and that was one reason I was there—to draw on my experience and knowledge of ministry among remote tribal cultures.

My first night in Suriname's interior was in the largest village of the Trio Indians. We slung our native hammocks in an open-sided house overlooking the river. I was thankful when a local elder checked the thatch and rafters overhead and deftly extricated a large tarantula, which he gently moved to a safe place—for its own sake, as well as ours! I only fell out of the hammock once that first night. Once was enough—I quickly learned how to use it and slept well until the air grew decidedly chilly, when I was glad of the light blanket Roy had told me to keep handy.

Our days were filled with meetings and times of worship. It was fascinating to sit with Asonko, the grand chief of the Trio people, who wore his rainbow-coloured feather headdress. Through Roy he explained the extent of his territory and the need to protect it from outsiders, especially illicit gold prospectors from Brazil. He was aware of the tension that existed between the preservation of the Trio way of life and hunting and fishing on the one hand, and the need for education, health care, and some measure of development on the other. Ironically, he had mixed opinions about an Amazon conservation group who had mapped out the Trio territory. The group assisted them in their struggle for land and natural resource rights, but was also involved in other ventures that he viewed with reservation, such as a tourism project and promotion of traditional medicine in cooperation with local shamans.

Asonko was also an elder in the church, so he sat with other leaders who told us of their concerns about the health of the church and new threats the community faced. Young people were increasingly affected by outside influences, especially when they made their way to the national capital or interacted with the occasional gold prospector or tourist. Later on, in a remote Wayana village, I saw what he meant when I watched two teenage boys dancing to a pop video on a cell phone!

One of the concerns raised by both Trio and Wayana church leaders was the sense that they needed more training—especially in how to study the Scriptures so they could "bring out the deeper truths" of the Bible, teach the people better and become more effective in pastoral counselling.

Roy and I discussed these issues at length with the people, and worked on a strategy that respected what they already knew and would not usurp their leadership, but rather strengthen and develop it. We also took into account the lifestyle of both groups, their geographical remoteness, and their linguistic and cultural isolation from churches, Bible schools and other Christian resources in the distant coastal capital.

This visit to Suriname was typical of my changing role in the mission. I wasn't deputed any more to visit churches and campuses for purposes of recruitment and raising support. The change had become more marked in 1995. Following the merger of RBMU with the former West Indies Mission that resulted in World Team, I was appointed to the training group for the World Team Institute of Church Planting. This was an annual month-long training event for field missionaries, and it became a many-layered blessing for me.

WIN, as we called it, gave me an opportunity to draw on my experience, research and studies in theology and missiology to help and encourage missionaries through teaching, informal group discussions and personal conversations. I also came to know dozens of enthusiastic and gifted people working in diverse places around the world. Some became particularly close and faithful friends, imitators of Christ who encouraged, challenged and provoked me in many constructive ways, so that these years proved to be among the richest in terms of my own spiritual journey.

Another consequence was that my colleagues appreciated my accumulated experience and the particular gifts and skills I had, and identified me as a trainer and mentor. Some even referred to me as the "resident missiologist"! Soon I was being asked to travel to places around the world, mostly rural or remote tribal areas, to help evaluate ministries, give training, guide strategies or suggest alternative methodologies.

Twice, I was invited to Cameroon, in the sweaty "armpit of West Africa," as the missionaries there like to describe it. "All of Africa is in Cameroon," I was informed. "We have savannah, semi-desert, rainforest, mountains and swamps. Everything that comes to mind when you think of Africa is found here."

I didn't get to see all that, but I travelled thousands of kilometers, often in four-wheel drive vehicles over dusty and rutted red dirt roads. On one occasion we barely avoided a heavily loaded logging truck which careened round a corner, taking up the whole road. Our alert driver missed it by inches by pulling in among the branches of a fallen tree on the side of the road.

I met and talked with leaders of the Cameroon Baptist Convention and saw firsthand innovative ministry among diverse groups such as the Baka pygmies of the rainforest in the southeast and the tall, elegant Fulani cattle herders in the northwest.

I was glad not only for my twenty years of experience in Papua, but also for the fact that both my parents and grandparents had been missionaries in the former Belgian Congo. To be able to say that I had that heritage and that I even had an African name—Bamenga—bestowed on me by the Lomongo people of central Congo, gave me credibility among the Cameroonians. The fact that I had also studied African Christianity at the feet of renowned Ghanaian theologian Kwame Bediako was not just a vain boast, it also meant I was better able to bring my experience and knowledge to bear in this African context, whether sitting with missionaries or the Cameroon Baptist Seminary professors.

In addition to travelling to fascinating new places like Suriname and Cameroon, I also continued to make regular visits to Indonesia. Arriving one time in Pontianak, the capital city of West Kalimantan, the familiar Asian humidity and pungent smell of clove cigarettes soon engulfed me as I stood in line in the airless immigration hall. Waiting my turn, passport in sweaty hand, I suddenly had cold feet. *What am I doing here?* I thought.

I had been invited by two friends and colleagues to help with a week-long church leader's seminar to be modelled somewhat on the style of our World Team Institute of Church Planting, although the focus was more on church life, discipleship and the pastoral role as outlined in the book of Ephesians. *I'm not qualified to do this,* I mused as I patiently awaited my turn. *Though I can get by with basic everyday Indonesian, I've always preached and taught using the Yali language.*

Finally, visa stamped, I emerged into the equatorial sun to be welcomed by my colleagues Dave Enns and Henry Armstrong. I told them my dilemma, but I didn't get the feeling that they took me too seriously. "You'll be OK!" they assured me, and Henry added, "If you get stuck, we can translate for you."

The seminar location was a large, bare-bones house on a beach, twenty kilometres south of the town of Singkawang. It had a spacious living/dining area with sparse bedrooms off each side and a simple kitchen separately at the back. Through double doors at the front, we stepped out onto the sandy beach flanked by coconut palms. Straight ahead was the inviting blue of the South China Sea. We lived together, sharing chores, eating together and gathering in a casual circle for the seminar meetings. The sound of the waves was constantly in the background and the sea breezes through the open doors and windows made the heat tolerable.

None of the men present knew who I was, and I could sense their reserve and even suspicion about having to listen to this stranger who had never lived in Kalimantan. After a faltering start, where I mixed up my pronouns and butchered the grammar, I apologized to the group of Dayak pastors. "I don't mean to insult you when I don't use the honorific titles properly or when I address you with the exclusive form for 'we.' Maybe I should speak in English and have Henry translate," I suggested.

"It is not a problem. We understand you, Pak John," they responded politely but warmly. I felt the ice had been broken by my vulnerability. "Please keep on going!"

Henry and Dave had asked me to speak on the spiritual dimension in Ephesians, and as I taught from chapter 1, the pastors came alive. When I connected the idea of their being "seated with Christ in the heavenly realm, far above all principalities and powers" with the realities they faced in the demonized world of Dayak culture, it made profound sense to them. By the end of the week, with my fluency improving and my teaching illustrated with pertinent stories and cultural anecdotes from Papua, I felt totally accepted and enjoyed a great rapport with them all.

The seminar was deemed a great success, and during the evaluation at the end, the Dayak church leaders were unanimous. "We have never attended a seminar like this before. We've been to some where you sit in rows and listen to lectures, get a nice tee-shirt and go home with a fancy manual which you never open again because it is not practical for Christian life and ministry. This is different. You sat with us. We talked together and shared our lives. This has touched our hearts and given us meaningful teaching and ideas we can take home and put into practice right away."

Dave and Henry had called the seminar "Semangat," which means zeal or enthusiasm in Indonesian, and we were blessed to see these men go home fired up with renewed passion for ministry. "Please do this again" was the general consensus.

Over a number of years my travels have taken me to several other countries in Africa, Latin America and Southeast Asia, and understandably some people envied the opportunities I had to travel and see the world. "Can't you put me in your suitcase?" a friend of mine asked umpteen times.

However, global travel in itself is not much fun. No matter where one goes, travelling is tedious, even though there are always beautiful things to see and fascinating sites to visit. What is immensely enjoyable, though, is to meet with Christian leaders from different cultures, discuss diverse issues, and encourage and help them. My broad experience, my studies, and the insights gained through Bible teaching and translation among the Yali people always reach people across cultural divides. Above all, I share the lessons learned in my own pilgrimage with Jesus. The venue doesn't matter. Whether at a conference in Taiwan, a seminar in Kalimantan, or in intimate conversation with a Yali in Papua, my passion is to encourage each disciple in his or her growing relationship with Jesus Christ.

CHAPTER 21

The Yali Story

"This is a story that must be told!"

Myles Lorenzen's voice was choked with emotion and tears welled up in his eyes as he held in his hands an open copy of the recently published Yali Bible and reverently turned its pristine pages. "In light of the history of Tyndale, Wycliffe and others like them, who laboured and suffered so much to give us our English Bibles, which we now take for granted, it is like leafing through a powerful piece of history for an entire, unique language group. A history that will impact people for generations to come."

Myles, one of my close American friends and a fellow trainer at WIN, had asked me to speak during his morning teaching session. I was not long back from Papua where this Bible—the first complete Bible in any of the 230 languages of Papua—had been publicly celebrated by the Yali people.

In my talk, I described the Bible dedication ceremony with its throngs of thousands of joyful and jubilant Yalis gathered in the open air. Groups of young people had spontaneously circled around, singing and dancing, and after numerous testimonies and speeches a representative of the Indonesian Bible Society formally presented a colourfully wrapped box of the Bibles to representatives of the Yali church.

After the ceremony, the Bibles were snapped up by eager purchasers who had been saving their rupiahs for months. In the ensuing weeks, I taught from the Old Testament. The people listened with excitement as the Bible came alive in their own language. One day, as I was teaching a group of church leaders from the story of Joseph in Genesis, we came to the part where his brothers explain to their father Jacob that Simeon was held hostage in Egypt, and to obtain his release they must return with Benjamin.

"My son will not go back to Egypt with you," Jacob declared vehemently. "His brother Joseph is dead, and Benjamin is the only one left. If any harm comes to him on your journey, you will send me gray-haired and grieving to my grave."[27]

As someone read these words aloud from the Yali Bible, I noticed a young man at the front sobbing, tears running down his cheeks and dropping onto the crisp, virgin pages of his new Bible. "Are you feeling all right?" I asked, wondering if perhaps he had his own personal sorrow.

27 Author's paraphrase, Genesis 42:38.

"No, I am okay," he assured me, "I am just moved as I read these words and realize exactly what Jacob must have been feeling!"

It was the same when I preached in the villages I visited. The churches were packed, and everyone who could read—men, women and children—had their new Bibles open in their laps as they sat cross-legged on the floor. There was an unusual silence; even the normally restless children and whimpering babies seemed to sense the import of the moment. In that stillness, as I preached, I heard the sound of rustling pages as people searched for the first time in the pages of the Old Testament.

"You should write a book," Myles had suggested. "It really is a remarkable story."

"But who would read it in the age of TV reality shows and tabloids? Maybe someone could make a video?" I mused aloud, then added, "Maybe I should talk to Dianne Becker."

Dianne was a documentary filmmaker and journalist who had taken a leave of absence from her job at a CBC affiliate TV station in St. Louis, Missouri. She wanted her sabbatical to be "a year to give back," and among other things had been using her time to make short video documentaries for a number of missionaries. She had decided to come to World Team's annual training event to gain an inside track not only on what missionaries do, but why.

I broached the subject of a video to Dianne and my video-savvy friend Doug Kracht, one of my fellow trainers at WIN. Before long, we were planning for a filming trip together to Irian Jaya towards the end of the following year, 2001. However, on September 11, 2001, I received a phone call that seemed to call the entire project into question.

"Are you watching the news?"

"No, I'm at my desk in the office. Why?"

"A plane just crashed into the World Trade Center in New York!"

It was my friend Doug calling me from Columbia, South Carolina to talk about my anticipated flight there the next day. We had planned this visit months ago to prepare a script and conclude planning for the filming with Dianne in late October. But by nightfall of 9/11, the ominous nature of the horrifying events and the haunting scenes of that fateful day had begun to sink into our brains, and we knew there would be no planes going anywhere in the USA. It seemed that our trifling plans were at least on hold and might need to be abandoned.

Nevertheless, the air routes soon reopened and we set out together across the Pacific in a half-empty plane. It was a long flight, with layovers in Kuala Lumpur and Jakarta before we arrived in Papua, where we processed a necessary travel permit in order to proceed to Wamena and then Holuwon. Gloria and our three sons joined us there a day or two later.

We stayed three full weeks among the Yalis, with most days spent filming dozens of hours of interviews, day-to-day activities, church services and a hut meeting. After capturing the video on their Mac computers, Doug and Dianne started work on editing while I began translating all the Yali and Indonesian interviews into English. I hadn't realized how much hard work this would be, and as the days went by, I became increasingly tired and felt the need to take a nap some afternoons. Sometimes I didn't feel well, but I kept going anyway because the job had to be done.

One night in the middle of the second week, I woke with acute abdominal pain. I couldn't find any way to get comfortable, whether I lay on one side or the other. Rather than disturb Gloria, I got up and went to the living room, where I found I could get some relief sitting in an old folding garden chair. Though the intense sharp pain lessened, it was obviously serious. I would have gone to the hospital if we had been at home, but in the middle of the night in the highlands of Papua, that wasn't an option. I wondered if it was appendicitis.

A few days earlier, we had been joined by a young Dani woman called Ami. I knew her parents because they had worked with us in Ninia back in the seventies. Her father Andreas had taken the family to Java where he entered a seminary and then stayed on doing evangelism and church planting in Muslim villages.

After high school, Ami had gone to Australia to study nursing. Following her return to Indonesia, she had married an educated Yali man and now lived in Wamena. She was fluent in English, so I had asked her to come and help record a voice-over in English.

In the morning, Gloria called Ami to come examine me. She poked and prodded me professionally, asking typical nurse-type questions. "No, Pak John, you don't have the classic symptoms of appendicitis, and the centre of your pain is not in the right spot. I am pretty sure you don't have appendicitis," she assured me. "However, you should start a course of antibiotics because you likely have some kind of infection."

This was the way we were used to dealing with medical issues when we lived at Holuwon, far from a doctor, and I didn't stop to think of an alternative possibility, especially as Dianne and Doug depended on me for transcribing the Yali interviews. As the day wore on, the pain began to ease and, preoccupied with the video filming, somehow I kept going. Within forty-eight hours the pain and discomfort had diminished. Obviously the antibiotics were working.

Eventually it was time for Doug and Dianne to set off home, while our family stayed on for a couple of weeks. Incredibly, Dianne had already completed the first draft of the video and we watched it together, amazed. It seemed surreal—like watching a documentary about unknown people and events—and yet there we were, telling our part in the story. But that was the point, it wasn't *our* story; it was the story of what God had done among the Yali people through the preaching, teaching and translation of his Word. When the video finally entered production, it was released under the title *The Yali Story.*[28]

Immediately after the filming, I headed to a place in the highlands called Pyramid where we were scheduled to hold a Semangat seminar. After conducting these training events in Kalimantan for several years, colleagues David Enns, Dave Martin and I were about to hold our second one in Papua. A few days earlier, however, as David Enns was on his way to Papua, his teenage son suddenly collapsed and passed away from a long-standing heart condition. It was decided that Dave Martin and I should carry on with the help of two leading Papuan pastors—Otto Kobak and Dorman Wandikbo.

The Semangat seminar got off to a good start, but sometimes I felt I lacked *semangat*—energy and zeal. My concentration and focus were lacking, and by each evening I was exhausted. I wasn't feeling well. Something wasn't right with my intestinal tract and I wondered if I had picked up some amoeba or bacterial infection. Fortunately, I was still on antibiotics after the painful episode in Holuwon. It was a precaution until I could see a doctor.

---

[28] The video *The Yali Story* went on to win awards and was translated into other languages including Arabic, Chinese and Indonesian. It was even broadcast to all Arabic- and Chinese-speaking regions of the world by satellite television.

In any case, I thought, *this seminar is only for a few days, and soon I'll be back in Canada where I can get everything checked out by my competent GP.*

Very early on Sunday morning, I got up and went to the bathroom, but since it was still dark and I felt a little feverish, I decided to go back to bed. Suddenly I doubled over and collapsed to the floor with an intense stab of pain—even worse than I had experienced in Holuwon. I crawled across the floor and somehow scrambled up onto the bed, clutching my knees to my chest and writhing in excruciating pain. It was too early to get help. No one was up. I just lay there in the dark, sweating and waiting for dawn.

At last I heard Dave moving about in the adjacent wooden cabin. "Dave! Can you hear me? I'm in pain," I called out as strongly as I could. "I need help!"

"I'll be there shortly, as soon as I get some clothes on!" he shouted back.

As soon as he checked me out, Dave fetched his son Kevin who was also attending the seminar as the mission's local field director. I had to tell Kevin my symptoms, because we had no radio or cell-phone contact with anyone. He had to ride his trail bike into Wamena and talk to a doctor on the phone or radio. This all took time, and it was not until mid-afternoon that a small Mission Aviation Fellowship plane came to Pyramid. I was strapped on a stretcher and airlifted across the mountains to a southern lowlands town called Timika.

It so happened at that time that our son Iain was working for a mining company in a nearby town, and Gloria and Malcolm were with him while I was at the seminar. Our greetings were too brief, as I was transferred from the Cessna to the waiting ambulance, but I didn't miss the concern and tears in their eyes.

The four-wheel-drive ambulance took me seventy kilometres up a mountain road that switch-backed up to an altitude of over two thousand meters, to the mining-town hospital. Originally the plan was for a helicopter to make the transfer, but the weather by this time of day made that impossible.

An experienced Australian doctor travelled with me in the ambulance, and on arrival at the hospital, helped with the process of admission, initial physical examination, X-rays, and blood work. Soon I was lying between crisp sheets in a private room with some kind of drip plugged into a vein. I was too sick and tired to bother about anything, and fell into a fitful sleep.

I was there for a week or so while more tests were conducted and my condition was stabilized, but they were not able to determine the problem. Meanwhile, the medical insurance company had arranged for me to be transferred yet again, this time to a hospital in Darwin, Australia. Once again, I was strapped into a Toyota

Land Cruiser ambulance, this time heading down the tortuous dirt road to Timika, where Gloria was waiting for me.

The next morning a small executive jet staffed by a doctor and nurse arrived from Australia to take us to Darwin. After strapping me in, checking my blood pressure and securing the drip, they signalled OK to the pilot, and soon we were off. As the wheels lost contact with the runway I wondered, *Is this the last time I will be in Papua? Was the filming of* 'The Yali Story' *my last legacy to the Yali people?*

CHAPTER 22

Under the Shadow

The days in Darwin became a blur. Admitted into a private hospital, I received outstanding care and yet, after the usual tests and a CT scan, there was still no clear diagnosis. However, one thing was evident: I was quite ill. I couldn't eat and was losing weight. Besides that, I found I couldn't read anything. It was becoming hard to focus my eyes and I couldn't concentrate. Even articulate prayer seemed impossible, yet I was communing with God and had a deep sense of his presence.

Drifting in and out of fitful sleep, I remember thinking about some books I had recently read about the Trinity and the idea that the Father, Son and Holy Spirit want to draw us into the joyful intimacy of their eternal fellowship—what one theologian calls "the Great Dance."[29] I understood this best from the way Jesus speaks about his own relationship with the Father and when he

---

[29] C. Baxter Kruger, *The Great Dance,* Percherosis Press, Jackson, Mississippi, 2000.

prays for his future disciples to be one "just as you, Father, are in me, and I in you, that they also may be in us."[30]

Though I found it hard to concentrate on reading my Bible or voicing thoughtful prayer, nevertheless I sensed the Father, Jesus and the Holy Spirit were with me and I with them in as real a manner as I was with Gloria sitting beside my bed. Though we didn't talk much, just as I knew her presence and her love, I knew theirs.

I don't know how many days I lay there, but one day the surgeon came to me and said, "Our diagnostics show us nothing specific, and even the CT scan and colonoscopy are inconclusive."

"I know there's something wrong," I insisted. "I feel constant pressure and tenderness in my lower abdomen."

The nurse pulled the screen around as the doctor folded down the covers and lifted my hospital gown. When he gently yet firmly palpated my abdomen, I felt his fingers linger over a particular spot. "Do you feel anything there?" he asked while exerting some downward pressure.

"I do!" I gasped.

---

30 John 17:21. *The Holy Bible,* English Standard Version, Crossway, Wheaton, Illinois, 2001.

"Then I'll tell you what I'll do, if you are willing. I'll do a laparoscopy. I'll go in through your belly button and if I see anything, we can proceed with the appropriate surgery."

I could see that the nurse was holding a clipboard with a pink consent form. "Give me the form and I'll sign it. Just do whatever has to be done." It didn't seem long before I was wheeled into the surgery, and the next thing I knew, I was back in the ward in a drugged haze with tubes sticking out of me and all kinds of people hovering around the bed. I could see one of them was Gloria, standing out of the way while the others went about their tasks.

What I didn't know till later was that things had been touch and go for a while because I had reacted negatively to the blood transfusion. Even when Gloria told me this I didn't appreciate how serious it was till I overheard a nurse comment to someone else, "We nearly lost him."

Then the pain set in. Deep throbbing pain. Pain that seemed beyond bearing despite the self-operated morphine pump a nurse had placed in my hand. "Just press it as often as you feel the need," she said. "Don't worry about overdosing yourself, because you won't!"

I was reluctant to pump it too often, though, and one day, or maybe it was the same day, I complained to God, "I feel as if I'm bearing all the pain of Darwin." I don't know what made me talk that way, but I heard his response, spoken with compassionate understanding and compelling conviction: "I know what you are feeling; I have borne the pain of the entire world."

Sometime later, I began to experience mild hallucinations. Usually they appeared like swirling swarms of little black insects, like fruit flies, and initially I thought that was what I was seeing. But one day the black cloud settled on the wall opposite my bed and took the shape of a leering, demonic face. "If this is just the morphine, Lord," I cried out in my heart, "help me put up with it; but if demonic power is behind it, send it away!"

As soon as I spoke the words, the black specks lost their ugly shape and started to leave the wall, changing into glittering gold, which drifted across the room and disappeared through the window. I didn't hallucinate again.

The surgeon had been in to see me a few times, and when he saw me awake, he sat down by my bed to tell me about the surgery. After inserting the laparoscope, he immediately explored the suspect area of my abdomen and found a large and fairly rare sarcoma, about the size of a big sweet potato, which had constricted the intestines. Not only he, but every doctor I saw subsequently was fascinated by the fact that this tumour was attached to the Meckel's diverticulum, a small appendix-like appendage on the small intestine.

"The tumour is what we designate a low-grade sarcoma and the possibility of metastasis is small. However, it does appear that it had ruptured earlier, and there were signs of previous bleeding. I resected part of your intestines, John, and am confident I got everything."

The tumour was sent to a pathology lab in Perth, and there the curiosity remains in a jar—no doubt of interest to medical students! In due time, I was fit enough to travel. Gloria had been in touch with the insurance company's international travel department in Vancouver, and one day I received a call. "We have your ticket, Mr. Wilson, to travel first class from Sydney through Honolulu to Vancouver, and then on to Toronto."

"What about getting from Darwin to Sydney?" I asked, presuming she had a ticket for that leg of the journey too.

"No, that's your responsibility, Mr. Wilson. Just take a taxi."

"Do you know how far it is from Darwin to Sydney? It's further than from Vancouver to Toronto!"

"Really!" she exclaimed in utter surprise. "We'll get back to you about that."

After a few unexpected hiccups, we finally arrived home in Canada in time for Christmas. I was more than twenty kilograms lighter than when I had left home at the end of October, but I soon started to put on weight again with all the good food and my renewed appetite. 2001 had been an eventful year.

As soon as possible, I checked in with my own doctor who arranged for me to see a top oncologist in Toronto early in the new year. I showed him all the results and reports from Darwin Hospital, and he confirmed everything I had been told by the surgeon there, assuring me again that the chance of metastasis was very slim. However, he arranged for me to have regular checkups at the oncology unit in our local hospital in Mississauga, Ontario.

About a year and a half later, I arrived early for my routine appointment and sat, relaxed, in the Oncology waiting room. I had already had the customary blood tests and CT scan a few days earlier and was reflecting on all my previous checkups which had confirmed everything continued to be normal, just as expected. When I was called in, it wasn't my regular oncologist, but instead, a young female intern. *That's a good sign,* I thought. *I'm such a routine case, he's handed me off to this young lady.*

In the examination booth she sat down opposite me. On her name tag I read "Dr. Elaine McWhirter." She said, "Mr. Wilson, I am sorry to tell you that the latest CT scan shows the cancer has returned. We see at least two small tumours." She added more information, but I was stunned, mixed thoughts and feelings clamouring for attention: dread, frustration and annoyance, and yes, faith and hope.

"Are you all right, Mr. Wilson?"

No, everything wasn't all right. For one thing, Gloria was away, visiting her ageing parents in England, and I would have to call her and let her know the news. Moreover, we had just completed plans to move to Singapore for a new ministry in southeast Asia, and had just agreed to rent our home to a family. There were tickets already purchased for Singapore that would have to be cancelled. And we had just received some large donations towards our move from supporting churches in England and Canada. There were so many things to take care of. I don't know how long I was silent before I answered, "No, I'm OK. It's just that in a couple of months we were going to move to Singapore, and now everything's changed."

I went home to an empty, lonely house. I phoned Gloria in London and my son Malcolm in Ontario. I e-mailed Jonathan in South Africa and Iain in Indonesia. Then I sent an e-mail circular to friends in Canada and all around the world. I cancelled our tickets to Singapore and phoned the family who was looking forward to renting our house.

On the phone, Gloria asked if I had called the pastor, and I had, but he neither prayed with me over the phone nor arranged to visit me. It was hard being forlorn and alone in a silent, empty house.

I looked up the latest information on this type of cancer on the Internet. It was discouraging. Yes, gastro-intestinal stromal tumours (GISTs) normally did not metastasize, but when they did the prognosis was not good. Perhaps within a year or two Gloria, my beloved wife of thirty-six years, might be a widow, my sons could be without a father, their children without a grandfather. I felt overwhelmed with sadness.

I found a piece of music which matched my melancholy—a recording of *Pavane Pathétique*, by Ludmila Knezkova-Hussey. A pavane is a slow and stately dance, and this composition was particularly soulful and moving. Ludmila had composed it in memory of her grandfather, a Czech violinist and composer, who had been brutally murdered some years earlier. It expressed Ludmila's grief and sorrow, and now I allowed it to help me give vent to my own inverted grief—not over a departed loved one, but over the loved ones I now expected to leave behind. I let the tears flow.

In those introspective days I read the Psalms and lingered reflectively over the story of David who was hunted by Saul, haunted by guilt over Bathsheba, and humiliated by his son when Absalom usurped the throne. The story became a kind of metaphor for me. I felt pursued by cancer, haunted by fear and apprehension, ousted by the cancer from the ministry I thought God had called me to. But like David I clung to the belief that it is God who "keeps my lamp burning."[31] Both life and ministry are his prerogative to give and to take.

I prayed. At times I longed passionately, like the Psalmist, for more intimate fellowship with God—to find refuge "under the shadow

---

[31] Psalm 18:28. *The Holy Bible,* New International Version, Hodder and Stoughton, London. 1979, 1986.

of his wings."[32] This did not refer simply, as I had supposed, to the wings of a bird protecting its young, but those overarching wings of the cherubim in the holiest part of the tabernacle, representing the holiest presence of God.

I assumed I would be having surgery again, and I remembered how I had experienced the enfolding sense of God's loving presence after the surgery in Darwin. *That's what I want to feel afresh*, I thought. *If the recurrence of this cancer can bring me that sense of intimacy with God, I can look forward to it with joy. I want to live under the mercy seat, under the shadow of his grace.*

In my reflections I also faced realistically the possibility of dying. *What if I only have eighteen months to two years of life left? How will I spend these remaining few months?*

Reading in Ephesians, which had become my favourite New Testament letter, some familiar words suddenly confronted me in a fresh way: "Watch the way you talk, and don't allow unwholesome words to escape your lips. Rather, you should focus on saying something fitting and constructive which will bring grace into the listeners' lives."[33]

Too often people found my analytical thinking and criticism discouraging and destructive, even when not intended that way. It is

---

32 Psalms 17:8; 63:7; 91:4.

33 Author's paraphrase, Ephesians 4:29.

too easy to be careless of the impact of our words and just speak our minds. We justify it by insisting that it is "the facts" or "the truth."

In another place, Paul says, "Knowledge makes people self-conceited whereas love builds up other people."[34] Knowledge gives power, but without grace and love, we become overconfident in our intellectual ability, and using it for self-advancement and proud ends, we become abusive and oppressive.

Yet the heart of the gospel is the sacrificial grace and kindness of God, which we not only receive, but which we can and should pass on to others in our words and deeds. Here in these challenging words in Ephesians, the apostle presents the possibility and necessity of passing grace on through our words. As I contemplated this, I was convicted.

I knew that my words, both spoken and written, though not necessarily unwholesome, had frequently upset and discouraged people. However, I noted that Paul was not only calling me away from that negative tendency, he was calling me to be positive, to be constructive, to use my words to impart grace to those who listened to me or read what I wrote.

I prayed, "Lord, my simple prayer and goal for whatever remains of my life is to intentionally seek ways to pass on your grace through my words."

---

[34] Author's paraphrase, 1 Corinthians 8:1.

CHAPTER 23

Intoxicated by Joy

It seemed like divine serendipity. The young doctor who broke the news that I had cancer again was also working with Canada's leading authority on gastrointestinal stromal tumours, Dr. Martin Blackstein. Later that same inauspicious day she called me to say that she had secured an appointment for me the following Tuesday at his regular clinic at Toronto's Mt. Sinai hospital. I soon came to realize I was in competent hands.

"There is a new treatment, a 'miracle drug' called Gleevec," he told me. "It was only recently approved by Health Canada, but in the trials, patients benefited from it greatly. It is not a cure, but hopefully it will significantly reduce your tumours and help control the cancer. However," he continued, "we cannot prescribe it until we are granted specific approval for your case, and it is also very expensive—about $3,000 a month."

As I waited to begin treatment, the three tumours grew astonishingly quickly and I was already experiencing considerable discomfort in my bloated abdomen and feeling the drain on my energy by the time the approval came through. Yet by the mercy of God and thanks to the favourable funding provisions of public health in Ontario, I eventually began treatment with this innovative oral chemotherapy. Within the first three months, the largest of the tumours had shrunk by as much as fifty percent. Three months later, I learned there was still progress, but the pace had slowed.

I think it was at my third follow-up that I cautiously asked the Jewish oncologist, "Is it all right for me to travel internationally?"

He knew I was a missionary because I had told him about my work and the fact that hundreds of Yali Christians, never mind other people, were praying for me. With good humour he asked, "Where do you plan to go? Back to Bongo-bongoland?"

"Yes, I want to go back to Irian Jaya, in Indonesia."

He hesitated, then with some reluctance spoke plainly. "You are aware of the risks from malaria and infections, but I suppose you know your options medically and the precautions you need to take. I wouldn't advise it, but I cannot prevent you."

This was sufficient blessing and encouragement for me. Nevertheless, I still had some apprehension as I planned the trip. I knew, for example, that there were certain antibiotics that were incompatible with Gleevec, so I had to ensure I had a supply of something suitable if it became necessary. For similar reasons, I couldn't take any malarial prophylactics, so I stocked up on DEET repellant and bought a new mosquito net which I impregnated with Permethrin.

So, after a lull in my travel to Papua following the emergency medical evacuation in November 2001, a new series of visits began. As the years passed, every three months I returned to the hospital in Toronto for a CT scan and the oncology clinic, and now Dr. Blackstein would ask, "How was your trip?" or "When are you going again?"

In addition to one or two annual trips to Indonesia, it was during this time that I also travelled to Cambodia, Hungary, the Philippines, South Africa, Singapore, Suriname and Taiwan. The amazing thing was that I always seemed to feel better afterwards. And all the while, I was still on Gleevec. I began looking ahead to 2011, which was going to be a landmark year. It was ten years since the filming of *The Yali Story* and my subsequent cancer surgery, but it was also forty years since Gloria and I had first set foot in Papua, not knowing what lay in store for us. Moreover, it was fifty years since the first missionary pioneers, Stan Dale and Bruno de Leeuw, had made the arduous hike over the mountains to gain a foothold for the gospel among the Yali people in the Heluk Valley.

The Yali people were looking forward to this milestone too. Tribal people traditionally live according to the memory of their personal and ancestral past, so it was not surprising that the older Yali

Christians were particularly intent on the younger generation understanding their history. "We know we have been brought from darkness to light, but our children have grown up only knowing the way we are now. We need to reiterate what it was like to live without knowledge of Jesus and the gospel. We need to emphasize what it was like to live in fear of the constant cycle of disease, death and natural disaster; to have our minds darkened by the untruths passed on from generation to generation by our ancestors; and to live perpetually in bondage to evil spirits. We need to show them how much our lives have been transformed by the Spirit of God, and we need to make sure the gospel is passed on from our generation to theirs."

For several months they planned and prepared to celebrate "Yubelium"—a Jubilee Festival. It was to be a celebration of the arrival of the gospel, on the anniversary of the arrival of Stan and Bruno in the Heluk Valley. It would be a regional event, with guests from other nearby tribes, the Hupla, Kimyal and Momina, invited to participate in the grand festival, because the gospel had spread out in ever-widening circles to reach their villages too. They also invited those of us who had followed in the footsteps of the pioneers and built on the foundations they had laid through teaching, discipleship, leadership training, literacy and Bible translation, and by serving their human needs with medicine, nutritional care and other humanitarian projects.

The main Jubilee celebration was a week-long series of events at Ninia, but Gloria and I, along with our sons and some of their family members, were invited to arrive early and spend a few days of joyful festivity with our friends at Holuwon.

When the MAF single-engine turboprop Kodiak plane landed and taxied to a stop, we could hear the vociferous singing of the welcoming crowd above the whine of the engine, and as we looked out we could see men, women and children dressed in colourful finery all around the top of the airstrip. As we climbed out, those designated to unload the plane and some of the pastors came out to greet us and "crown" us with feather circlets.

For an emotion-filled moment, we stood still, taking in the scene. There were two main groups. One was the general crowd led by pastors and elders. The other was the women's fellowship group whose leaders were attired in colourful Papuan batik dresses and bedecked with headdresses of brilliant feathers of birds of paradise, parrots and parakeets. We choked back welling emotion as we listened to each choral group sing specially composed songs that recounted the coming of the gospel to Holuwon and specifically mentioned Gloria and me by name.

Then we were ushered towards the path that climbed from the airstrip up to our house. It was lined with women and girls dressed in their most colourful clothes, with newly woven, multicoloured net bags hanging down their backs. As we moved forward, we were preceded by a rainbow wave of movement as, one by one, they swung their bags from their heads to spread them on the ground in front of us. It was an extraordinary token of honour and respect, and we felt (as was intended) that we were treated like Jesus.

In the next few days we spent many hours just talking with old friends. We enjoyed listening to dozens of newly composed hymns in the traditional and unique, polyphonic style of the Yali. My son Jonathan and I spoke in special seminars and finally, on Sunday, we participated in a large open-air worship service attended by representatives of all the area villages.

On Monday morning the family was flown by MAF plane up-valley to Ninia for the week of festivities there. The massive six-day celebration was beautifully orchestrated, with times of worship including testimonies, choirs and specially composed hymns. There were teaching seminars for church leaders and those in secular employment, youth meetings, a concert, and a baptism of well over a hundred youths as well as gray-haired men and women, which attested to the continuing discipleship and growth of the Yali church.

Pervading the entire series of events was an atmosphere of joyful praise and thanksgiving, with the regular affirmation: "Nenakni Allah neg motdeg welamag!" (Let God alone be glorified). The whole glorious occasion had been designed to celebrate the goodness, power and grace of God in delivering the Yali, the Hupla, the Kimyal, the Momina and others from the powers of darkness. "Now we are walking in the light," they declared.

They also celebrated having the Scriptures translated into each of their languages. In the preceding twelve months the Kimyal and the Momina had received their New Testaments, the work on the Hupla Bible was being readied for publication, and the Yali community was standing by for a new edition of their Bible—all the existing stock was sold out and many had copies that were dog-eared and worn.

Everyone in the crowds sang their hearts out with hymns ancient and modern. It was moving to hear the full-voiced renditions of old hymns translated by Stan Dale and Bruno de Leeuw, and we saw the people's unrestrained emotions as they sang new compositions, some composed especially for the occasion. Joyful tears flowed, hands gave expression to the words, and feet and bodies moved to the rhythms.

At the opening service, I was asked to pray. As I prayed and thanked God for his salvation, the hundreds, maybe thousands, at the outdoor gathering erupted with spontaneous applause and whoops of joy. We had never heard anything like it, and we were not alone.

After the prayer the master of ceremonies commented, "We have never done that before—it is not our custom. But today we responded with spontaneous joy to all that God has done. To God alone be the glory!" This led to more applause, accompanied by further excited whoops and whistles.

Finally the Jubilee concluded with a public declaration in which various leaders led the gathered community in a collective commitment to continue to be faithful to the gospel entrusted to them during the past fifty years, and to participate in taking it into the world.

Like any church, the Yali church is not without its problems, but this most recent event gave evidence of genuine spiritual life, hope and missionary vision. Over forty years, Gloria and I had witnessed, and in some small way participated in a wonderful movement of God. We saw hundreds of Yali people turn to Christ. We learned their language and stumbled into Bible translation. We helped them learn to read and write and become effective literacy teachers. We grappled with understanding their culture and tried to help them grow in their understanding of God's Word. We trained church leaders and even dabbled in medicine and community development.

Not many missionaries have the chance to stand at the fifty-year point and assess what has been accomplished, evaluate how the various mission endeavors have helped shape the church and see where it now stands with promise and hope. Having done so, all I can do is echo the words voiced many times during the Jubilee celebrations, "To God alone be the glory."

Praising God at the Jubilee celebration

EPILOGUE

Later in the Jubilee year, I went back to Papua for another Semangat seminar. It was quite a low-key event compared to the grand celebration at Ninia. No one came with feather headdresses! More importantly, none came with an "attitude." The gathering consisted of a handful of humble and unpretentious pastors and their wives who represented several highland communities and usually monolingual tribal churches. A few came from "city" churches where they ministered to mixed congregations including well-educated Papuans from diverse tribes as well as Indonesians from other islands. All were eager to learn from the Scriptures. Each brought good questions and all contributed thoughtfully to the discussions.

One of the participants was a gray-haired Dani man whose face looked familiar, but I couldn't place him. As we went around the room introducing ourselves, he seemed to look straight at me as he said, "My name is Nainal Kogoya."

Immediately, I remembered him. He had been a shy teenager accompanying the missionary who had welcomed us when we first arrived in Papua forty years earlier. Now he was a pastor of one of the largest Dani churches in the Tolikara regency and served a congregation of several hundred.

Papua has come full circle. The evangelical churches are now sending teams to plant new churches in other parts of Indonesia and expect to be going further afield in the near future. One senior church leader commented to me, "The gospel has come all the way from Jerusalem to Irian Jaya; now we must take the gospel back to Jerusalem!"

Soon after this I returned to Canada for another routine check-up at the oncology department. For a few moments, Dr. Blackstein looked carefully and silently at the latest CT scan and the radiologist's notes. His face was inscrutable, and there was a moment of suspense as I awaited his fresh diagnosis.

"The radiologist and I are in total agreement, John," he began. "There is no longer any discernible evidence of the cancer. It means that after over eight years of treatment you now are officially in remission!"

"Wasn't it the case," I asked, "that back then the prognosis was that I had about two years to live?"

"The median survival rate is still two years," he replied.

As he spoke, I recalled my first meeting with him. He already knew I was a Christian missionary, and I had told him, "I have many friends praying for me all around the world, including hundreds of the Yali people where I used to work."

He had made no comment, but as the months had become years and I continued to grow healthier, on several occasions he'd said, "John, your case is quite remarkable. You have made amazing progress!"

As I drove home from that appointment, I reflected on my life over the last ten years. Without a doubt, it had been astounding. I had been given more years and a better quality of life than I expected. In many ways, this phase of my life now seemed to have been more significant than those very exciting and satisfyingly productive years in Papua. It had been a period of reassessment, an inner journey through which I came to know myself better and during which I began to value the quality of personal relationships more than outward success or tangible achievement. It had become more important to me to reach out to people, to encourage and influence them as they faced changes and challenges in their own lives, to give them hope when they were confronted by suffering or tragedy.

Occasionally people have asked me about cancer and the place of suffering in our lives. Some obviously see it as unnecessary as well as fundamentally evil. We have all heard people say, "If God is a God of love, how can he allow suffering?"

Others have voiced another concern: "John, how could God allow you to have cancer twice after serving him as a missionary and doing so much good?"

All these questions betray some debatable suppositions. I wonder what kind of God they have in mind. It seems to me that the God of their imaginations is unlike the God who is revealed to us in the Bible—the God and Father of Jesus Christ whom I have come to know. I meet many who assume on the one hand that a loving God is incompatible with suffering, and on the other that affliction can have no constructive purpose in anyone's life. They also suppose that somehow pain or sorrow of any kind is a kind of curse, and certainly not just deserts for anyone who lives a "good life." It also seems they think that if God loves us at all, afflictions and suffering in some way put limits on his loving care and protection or ultimately cut us off from God's love.

My experience convinces me the opposite is true. Nothing can separate us from God's love. No one and nothing in all creation can come between us and God's love. No affliction or hardship, no sickness or tragedy, no hatefulness, bullying or maltreatment and no demonic or earthly power can prevent us from experiencing God's love. In fact, these circumstances can become the opportunity to experience God's love and grace in a new way. It is God, through his love, who turns adversity into unanticipated good, makes our trials the forge of strong character, and above all, strengthens our faith and justifies our hope.[35]

Surely the inner journey of mind and spirit, then, is as important if not more so than our outer physical existence. If we fail to

---

35 Author's paraphrase, Romans 5:1-5 and 8:28-39

examine that inner world, we remain victims of our past. We become captive to our present adverse circumstances and live constrained by uncertainty and fear of the future. Surely if we foster a trusting relationship with God, it is possible by faith, love and hope in his sovereign and faithful goodness to become people who rise above disadvantage, adversity and personal failure.

By my reckoning, these latter years have been unusually and unexpectedly good because I experienced and proved God's presence, love and grace in the midst of adversity. In retrospect, I feel my whole life has been amazingly blessed. I am able to look back on my childhood as infused with much happiness, joy and benefit. My adult years were like an apprenticeship in living—learning on the go from all kinds of artisans in many different spheres.

Not many have enjoyed the unique experiences I have had since I left Scotland over forty years ago to travel to far-off places, make my home in an exotic land, interact with, learn from and make friends with people fresh from the "Stone Age," and even experience the grief and pain of cancer. Some might not even want to have some of those experiences, but I am a richer man for my pilgrimage in these other worlds.

CPSIA information can be obtained at www.ICGtesting.com
Printed in the USA
LVOW07s0416300115

424925LV00002B/50/P

9 781490 855530